ONE WEEK LOAN

making THE LOWRY

LOWRY PRESS

making | THE LOWRY

JEREMY MYERSON   PHOTOGRAPHY BY LEN GRANT

Publishing and editorial direction:
Roger Sears

Edited by Michael Leitch

Designed by Hemisphere

Published by the Lowry Press
The Lowry
Pier 8 Salford Quays
Greater Manchester M5 2AZ

First published 2000
© The Lowry Centre Limited, 2000

ISBN 1 902970 04 7

Reprographics by Principal Image

Printed and bound in Spain by Imago

CONTENTS

FOREWORD

A former leader of Salford City Council once said, "If I've got to sup wi' devil to do well by the people of Salford, I'll sup wi' devil." He never revealed whom he had in mind, and we can only guess. But the story of The Lowry is the story of a few people's vision, personal courage and willingness to go to almost any lengths with the odds constantly against them.

The Lowry was not someone's pet passion, a monument to civic vanity or a scheme dreamt up by a local authority to get "our fair share of Lottery money". It was the culmination of a long and carefully researched regeneration project. Salford needed better housing, schools and jobs. An international landmark arts complex was a credible way to unlock the jobs and inward investment needed. But imagine the courage it took to pursue such an ambitious scheme when surrounded by so many pressing problems. Local people quickly grasped the potential, but outside Salford there was scepticism bordering on derision.

Those responsible for the capital funding of this project have sought to test the proposition of The Lowry well beyond the point of initial appraisal and approval for funds. They are right to have been rigorous in their examination of a scheme as expensive and ambitious as The Lowry. No project has been more scrutinised, though if you continually pull up the plant to see if the roots are growing, there is a danger that you end up killing the very thing you are trying to nurture.

Perhaps you have to be hardy to flourish in the North. Salford's bravery extended to handing over control of The Lowry to an independent Trust and a team of professional managers, to give it the best possible chance of success. They kept a close watch but they let go - like any good parent.

The Lowry has already delivered substantial numbers of jobs and inward investment. The people who started it wanted to do something much more difficult - to say to local people, "Salford can attract, and has a right to expect, the very best." The Lowry has done that too. Michael Wilford's building has attracted international acclaim.

In the end, those who believed in The Lowry and all it stands for proved more determined and resourceful than its doubters and detractors. We found friends at the highest levels of both a Tory and a Labour government, and among public servants. The teams who designed, built and now operate it, are an exceptional bunch of highly talented people, prepared to work as long and as hard as it takes to succeed. The only prima donnas in this project will be on the Lyric Theatre's enormous stage.

But the real stars are the generations of Salford councillors, their officers and their people, who had the foresight not only to recognise the talent of L S Lowry, but the courage to find and pursue a radical solution to inner-city deprivation. It is, perhaps, in the nature of those who invest public funds in major projects that they treat the local authority as the sole "beneficiary", even though the benefits and impact are regional and national. One day someone, somewhere, will say "thank you" to Salford for having had the courage, and taken the risk, to create Britain's landmark Millennium project for the Arts. This book goes some way to placing on record the trials, tribulations and triumphs of an extremely complex project. Unlike many such books, it extends the discussion of design and construction and their realisation into other areas, involving broad-ranging ideas about the arts, culture, marketing, education and creativity. The book, like The Lowry, has something in it for all of us.

FELICITY GOODEY

CREATING THE VISION

"Look at the sky, look at the water, this could be
a wonderful dockside development...."

Peter Hunter, architect and town planner

Previous page: Aerial view of
Salford docks, photographed
by the German Luftwaffe in
the Second World War -
they planned a destruction
that actually took place just a
few decades later.

An aerial view of Salford Quays in the industrial North-West of England on a clear spring day early in the new millennium. Rising above the neat patterns of a regenerated urban dockland area, with its mix of homes, offices and leisure facilities, is a large and unusual collage of light modern structures sited at a dynamic point close to the water. This is The Lowry, a new showcase for the performing and visual arts which is among Britain's first exceptional public buildings of the 21st century. For all its modernity, The Lowry looks as though it has always belonged here. Its design has absorbed the history and landscape of the site, creating the most significant development for the City of Salford since the construction, more than a century before, of the Manchester Ship Canal on which it sits.

This is no monolithic and forbidding temple of culture. Its foyers and promenades throng with people. From the air, one is tempted to describe them as matchstick men, but the open, bright setting is as far removed from the dark, grimy, industrial landscapes of L S Lowry's Salford factory paintings as it is possible to be. A band is playing in the sun. The layers of the building reveal the activity inside. Away from the public's gaze, lorries are unloading sets and costumes for a major touring production. Musicians unpack their instruments. At the tip of the pier, The Lowry's interlocking architectural forms tilt at the boats passing by.

To the south, a new lifting footbridge of radical design links The Lowry to Trafford Park Wharfside and the site of the new Imperial War Museum - North. To the west, an extension of the Metrolink connects The Lowry via a rapid light tram system to Manchester city centre. Construction workers meanwhile toil on a smaller building next to The Lowry, the Digital World Centre, which will present the burgeoning world of the new digital technologies. Surveyors in hard hats point and plan as an adjacent commercial shopping and leisure development also takes shape. This is the Lowry Galleria, which will sit in front of The Lowry and contribute revenue to its funding.

A symbol of renaissance

The Lowry opened in April 2000, taking audiences for the first time into its main 1,730-seat Lyric Theatre and smaller, adaptable 466-seat Quays Theatre; into its galleries for the L S Lowry collection and exhibitions; into its Artworks Gallery, which explores the nature of creativity; into its public spaces, bars and cafés. To have visited the site just a decade before would have been to see nothing of all this, only to witness cautious infrastructure improvement in the face of dereliction. To have been here 20 years before, in the early 1980s, would have been to confront industrial decline on a grand scale, an abandoned and stinking dock, all hope seemingly abandoned too.

The renaissance of Salford Quays, which The Lowry symbolises, has been achieved in the face of considerable scepticism. Who would have thought that a major national arts project, one of Britain's flagship millennium projects, innovatively funded by several different parties at a total cost in excess of £90 million, could be achieved in a place of such uncompromising economic hardship? Who would have thought the arts could take such a prominent role in a local community fighting long-term social deprivation? When the first masterplan for The Lowry was unveiled by architects James Stirling and Michael Wilford in 1992, the *Guardian* architectural critic Deyan Sudjic wrote: "If it gets built, it will be as if a transport café has, by some unexpected miracle, been given three Michelin stars but kept its original clientèle."

Now The Lowry has been built and its clientèle includes the local community as well as people from across the North-West of England and much further afield. It has opened its doors, not as a result of some unexpected miracle but due to the skill and hard work of an entire cast of characters whose efforts and insights have been marshalled by The Lowry Project team under the direction of chief executive Stephen Hetherington. "The Lowry does not have a single function any more than a town has a single function," explained Hetherington. "It is a collection of vistas, atmospheres and activities which reflects a view of artistic creativity as about the relationship between human beings and their world."

How it was done

This book sets out to tell the complete story of the making of The Lowry: how it was conceived, planned, developed and funded; how it was designed, engineered and constructed; how it was branded, marketed, programmed and prepared for opening. It is a chronicle of twists and turns, setbacks and triumphs. It has its roots in a vision for the urban regeneration of the Salford Quays skilfully nurtured by Salford City Council, and its narrative unfolds in the myriad decisions and actions of all those individuals and companies who contributed to the project at different stages. These included Salford City Council officers, professional consultants and contractors, Lowry Project directors and the Lowry Centre Trust. It is their interaction that gives the story of The Lowry its momentum. Ultimately, it is their commitment in the face of sometimes overwhelming odds that gives The Lowry story a successful conclusion, which is also a beginning. As Felicity Goodey, chairman of The Lowry Centre Trust, observed: "We had the ability to laugh at ourselves, admit when we were wrong and learn from our mistakes. That saw us through."

Some aspects of the making of The Lowry are generic to all schemes of this type in terms of the arts and design management processes involved: the need to coordinate and balance the inputs of different consultants, to keep the funders updated and onside, to construct a business model which dictates the functional aspects of the building as the scheme develops, to build brand awareness, and to avoid "white elephant" syndrome. All of these things are discussed. But other aspects reviewed here are unique to this special project and to this site. The urban regeneration strategies introduced at Salford docks have been seen elsewhere on waterfront sites in Britain and other parts of the world, but it is the particular context of Salford - the city, the community and the council, and what it went through to realise The Lowry - which gives the story its edge.

The narrative I have woven is based on interviews with the key people involved in the project, regular visits to the site, study of literature and documents relating to the making of The Lowry dating from historic social archives to the latest design blueprints, and my own long-term interest in the role of the cultural building in urban regeneration. In 1996 I published a book called *New Public Architecture* which described 50 outstanding works of public architecture around the world built in the early 1990s. Many were arts buildings constructed to revitalise areas affected by industrial decline. The Lowry compares favourably with these exemplars of design for change and would sit well in their illustrious company.

Manchester Ship Canal

To understand the scale of the problem and the specific achievement at Salford, it is necessary to go right back to the beginnings of the site - and the opening of the Manchester Ship Canal by Queen Victoria in 1894. This was a feat of engineering, running from Eastham on the Mersey Estuary to Salford - a length of 35.5 miles. It enabled sea-going vessels of up to 12,500 tonnes to sail right into Greater Manchester and the industrial heartlands of the North-West, and was built at a time of great national confidence when Britain was the workshop of the world. Significantly, the Manchester Ship Canal opened just five years before Queen Victoria laid the foundation stone of the Victoria and Albert Museum in London, so setting the seal on an era of unprecedented industrial prosperity. Another Royal visit to the Manchester Ship Canal in

Below: Edward VII's Royal
visit to the Manchester
Ship Canal, 1905.

Bottom: Salford docks as a
busy hub of industrial Britain.
Pier 8 in the centre of the
picture was destined to be
the site of The Lowry, and the
patch of land at foreground
right would be allocated
to the Imperial War
Museum - North.

1905 by Queen Alexandra and King Edward VII marked the opening of No 9 dock - the area on which The Lowry stands today.

With its new canalside docks, the city of Salford, a prominent site of the Industrial Revolution in the early 19th century, was destined to grow rapidly. In 1896, nearby Trafford Park Industrial Estate was opened for the manufacture and export of textiles and machinery and the whole area boomed. At its mid-20th century peak, Trafford Park employed 75,000 workers. Salford veterans recall thousands upon thousands of men and women streaming into its factories every day. Salford had experienced a major increase in population, from 7,000 to 220,000 by the early years of the 20th century, but even amid enormous wealth creation and with a massive labour force in work, social and economic conditions were often appalling.

In common with the area's other traditional industries such as engineering and steel-making, Salford's docks suffered terrible decline at the end of the 1960s. The advent of containerisation, shifts in trade patterns and the increase in the size of ships all affected Salford badly. The glory days were over and worsening economic conditions, precipitated by the oil crisis of 1973 and subsequent industrial unrest in Britain, speeded up the rate of decline. By the late 1970s, the loss of trade and jobs in the North of England was alarming and the once-proud docks of inner Salford, by now squalid and polluted, qualified to receive derelict land funding under the British Government's Urban Programme.

Enterprise Zone

When the Conservative Government was elected in 1979, urban policies changed and Enterprise Zones were introduced. A Salford/Trafford Park Enterprise Zone was set up in August 1981, encompassing some 150 hectares, the majority being vacant land owned by the Manchester Ship Canal Company and held for port expansion purposes. But although some dock areas were still considered operational at that time, the savage economic recession of the early 1980s signalled the end. Salford docks closed forever in 1982 and its wharfside sheds were targeted for demolition. A giant grain elevator which also needed to go symbolically defied several attempts to blow it up. Reluctant to lose its once-solid position on the docks and be consigned to history, this leaned precariously for months, like a concrete Tower of Pisa, attracting many curious visitors.

There was little else inviting about the plight of Salford docks, or in the local area for that matter. Jobs at Trafford Park nose-dived towards an all-time low of 24,500 by 1985, as unemployment in the North-West soared above 30 per cent in some places. Salford City Council chief executive John Willis, who had joined the council in 1966, recalled how bad things were at the time: "All the traditional industries were shutting and we faced this urban wasteland right in the middle of the city. Unlike Liverpool or London, the docks didn't have good warehouse buildings that could in time be renovated. The challenge was what to do with the docks and the Council took the view that it had to do something. And that meant partnership with the private sector."

Under the Conservatives, Enterprise Zones were intended to provide tax breaks, capital allowances and simplified planning procedures so that private investment could help to redevelop urban areas of social deprivation. The new political ideology of the time was that market forces and private capital could solve everything and many Labour-run local authorities were automatically hostile to this. But, faced with its rotting docks and frequent factory closures, Salford needed to be pragmatic. It sought alliances which, in retrospect, were politically courageous and ahead of the thinking at the time. Les Hough, the then Council leader, described it as "supping with the devil" but nevertheless this tenacious character was central to building bridges with former ideological enemies.

The City Council had already been brave in selling off Salford's worst tenement blocks to private housebuilders for nominal sums to redevelop as owner-occupier flats. Now it persuaded the Department of the Environment to allow it to purchase the docks and engage private entrepreneurs and developers in a phased programme of dockland regeneration. In late 1983 it acquired the majority of the docks (about 90 hectares) from the Manchester Ship Canal Company for a reputed £1.5 million. It then reached agreement with private developer Ted Hagan's Urban Waterside company to transfer land around Dock 6 to its ownership on condition that at least £4.5 million of private sector development be secured. Meanwhile, derelict land funding from the Urban Programme enabled work to start on reclamation as well as new services, landscaping and roads. Hagan's plan was for a cinema and hotel to occupy the site. Salford was about to begin the long march back from the brink. "At the City Council, we had sleepless nights over the guarantees we had to give but they were never called on," said Willis. "Investment from the Government's Urban Programme and its Derelict Land Programme, together with our own budget, meant we were eventually able to start sorting out the infrastructure."

A guiding figure

Around this time, an architect and town planner destined to become a powerful influence on the development of The Lowry arrived on the scene. His name was Peter Hunter and he was a partner in an architectural firm called Shepheard Epstein Hunter which had worked extensively with local authorities in the 1960s building new universities, and had subsequently developed an expertise in urban redevelopment at London Docklands. Hunter had joined the practice in the early 1960s, becoming a partner in 1966. He explained: "We designed university campuses at Lancaster, Warwick, Keele and Liverpool. As planning exercises, they were like little urban towns and they taught me a great deal. But by the end of the 1970s, things were traumatic for architects: the mandatory fee scale was discontinued, the profession was in disarray and the recession meant no work. We began casting around for new things to do. That's when we became involved in London's Docklands."

In 1981, at virtually the lowest point in the fortunes of Salford docks, Hunter attended an exhibition held at Centrepoint in London on the subject of Enterprise Zones. There he met

Peter Hunter, architect and town planner: an early enthusiast for the potential of the site.

by chance Salford's industrial development officer Peter Henry, who issued a blunt challenge: "Be in my office in Salford at 9am next Monday and I'll show you around." Hunter was intrigued and made the trip. "I suppose Peter Henry wasn't expecting that I would show up, but I did," recalled Hunter. "I immediately thought - what a wonderful site. Seeing such big ships appearing at an inland location as if through fields was surreal. I later learnt that the original engineer of the Port of Manchester was a man named Henry Hunter, so perhaps there was a sense of destiny in our meeting."

Shepheard Epstein Hunter worked speculatively on the project for a couple of years, offering suggestions and advice as Salford City Council set about purchasing the docks and assessing options for redevelopment. By 1984 it was clear to Salford's deputy chief executive Mike Shields that if private investment was to be attracted on a sufficient scale then a Development Plan for the area was needed to provide direction, clarity and reassurance. That year, a town planner called Tony Struthers joined Salford City Council and immediately saw the problem: "Salford Quays was derelict. It was evident we weren't going anywhere. We needed a concept." Shepheard Epstein Hunter was commissioned to prepare a blueprint to transform the former docks into an environment where people would want to live, work and play. Ove Arup and Partners were appointed consulting engineers. Struthers, a meticulous and energetic man who is today director of development services and deputy to John Willis at Salford City Council, played a key role on the project team.

The first Development Plan

The Salford Quays Development Plan was published in April 1985. In its Foreword, Roger Rees, Salford's chief executive at the time, pulled no punches: "The trade and jobs have gone; the land and water remain and, if left to rot, would have a devastating effect on surrounding areas for years to come. That cannot be allowed to happen." Heralding a "bold, exciting and imaginative plan", Rees and Struthers introduced a document which set out a reclamation programme concentrating on the three most important aspects of the site: water; roads and services; and public access and landscape. The plan sought to create "a new quarter of the City which has a unique character derived from the way in which all parts of the development are related to water. Some places should be vast and urban, other places should be very closed-in, secluded."

The plan identified the main views, vistas and external spaces, and created three areas in detail to show what could be achieved. Most importantly, it specified a mixed-use development: one-third business; one-third residential and one-third leisure. It ruled out heavy industry, hypermarkets and warehousing for the area, focusing instead on the prospect of leisure attractions, even a dockside museum. Although there was no specific proposal for an arts centre, the first seed of The Lowry had been sown.

A significant encounter

The sense of direction provided by the Salford Quays Development Plan had exactly the galvanising effect that Tony Struthers intended. The Department of Environment gave the green light to a rolling programme of work to improve the site in terms of infrastructure, services and environmental enhancements. At the same time, private sector investment around Dock 6 began to take shape in the form of a cinema, hotel, offices and housing.

Something else happened of immense long-term significance to the making of The Lowry, but nobody knew it at the time. To obtain media coverage for Salford Quays which might spread the word to private business in the North-West of England, Salford's industrial development officer

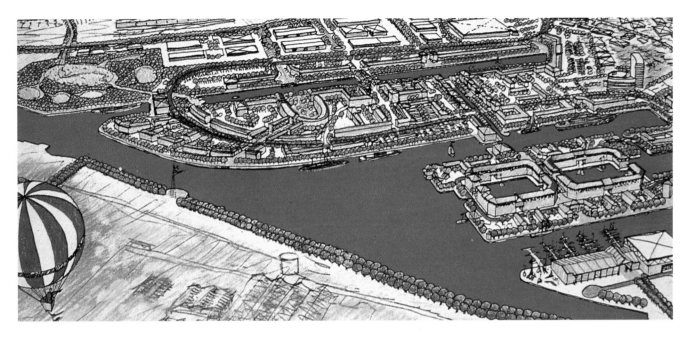

Peter Henry invited a BBC journalist he knew to visit the docks and interview Peter Hunter of Shepheard Epstein Hunter. That journalist was the BBC's Northern industrial correspondent Felicity Goodey. By the early 1980s she was a well-known face in the region on account of her TV appearances on *Look North* - she had been covering Salford industrial issues since the early 1970s. "I took a TV crew to the docks," recalled Goodey, "and there was Peter. 'Look at the sky, look at the water, this could be a wonderful dockside development,' he said. I did a piece to camera but I had to redo it twice because the crew were falling about laughing at his vision. Given the state of the place, it just sounded ludicrous."

Felicity Goodey knew perhaps better than anyone else just how far Salford had fallen, but she was impressed by the City Council's determination to improve the area, and by its imagination and flexibility, and she was willing to accentuate the good news wherever she could find it. The trouble was that there was little good news around. "When I first arrived in the area it was like stepping back in time to the early years of the Industrial Revolution," she recalls. "Salford was always the poor relation of Manchester, full of tenement housing in terrible condition. A place of poverty but also a fascinating place which produced an astounding variety of talented people, from Faraday in science to Albert Finney in the arts. The first public lending library was in Salford. The first family planning clinic was in Salford. The Vegetarian Society was founded in Salford. But by the 1970s, when I came on the scene, the focus was on deprivation, poverty, picket lines and strikes. It was all *Cathy Come Home* and *Coronation Street*."

When Goodey went to cover yet another strike, Salford City Council, weary of battling against negative media coverage, refused to cooperate. "So I made a deal with them. I would do my best to cover positive stories without ignoring the bad news. I wanted to make my base in the

Visions of the future from the Salford Quays Development Plan, April 1985.

Top: Aerial view of the docks.

Above: View through the canal.

Right: Plans showing how the docks would be developed.

CONSTRUCT DAMS

ROUTE OF SURFACE WATER

QUAY EDGE PEDESTRIAN ROUTE

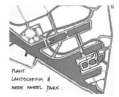

PLANT LANDSCAPING & MODE WHEEL PARK.

North-West and I couldn't afford to have no-go areas as a journalist. That deal led me directly to Salford docks in spring 1985 and my first meeting with Peter Hunter." It turned out to be a very significant encounter. A decade later, Goodey would be thrust into the frontline of the fight to build The Lowry as the project's champion and chairman of The Lowry Centre Trust, her role switching dramatically from reporter on the sidelines to leading player in the thick of the action.

But that development in the plot would be some time ahead. Back in 1985, Goodey filed her BBC story on the Salford Quays Development Plan, turned freelance and went off to live in Italy for a couple of years. Her contacts at Salford City Council promised to stay in touch and keep her informed of future developments on the Quays.

Improving the site

These developments came thick and fast. Between 1986 and 1991, a programme of public sector works proceeded at a rapid pace. The site was cleared, bunds (embankments) constructed, canals and bridges built, roads and services developed, trees planted, walkways laid out, the water cleaned and stocked with fish, street furniture and safety equipment installed, and a railway swing bridge and two redundant cranes were refurbished and relocated. Materials from the demolished concrete wharfside sheds were reused to dam the water between the newly formed quays and the Ship Canal. In all, reclamation and infrastructure contracts worth around £30 million were awarded by the City Council project team, advised by Shepheard Epstein Hunter and Ove Arup. Urban Programme and Derelict Land Grant funding from the Government, and later from the European Regional Fund, covered the cost, sending a message of growing confidence about the future of the area to private developers.

Cleaning the water

One of the most interesting aspects of this programme was the treatment of the polluted water. For those who remembered a stinking canal filled with the detritus of industry, the discovery of

fish swimming in the cleaned and oxygenated waters of the Quays was nothing short of a miracle. Dockers at Salford called it "the black dock" - with good reason. The standard joke was "the only fish that come out of this water are in tins!" Yet, through a process of isolation and aeration to create "zones" of oxygenated water in the dock basins which could support fish and acquatic life, experts managed to create one of the largest inland fisheries in the UK.

The scale of the problem they faced was immense. According to biologist Dr Bill Bellamy of APEM, a consultant on the project, "The samples we took from the sediment at the bottom of the canal were very revealing. Halfway down were hydrocarbons from the petrol used at the beginning of the Industrial Revolution. Further up we even found cotton fibres. It was just like the rings of a tree. You could see the whole history of the Manchester Ship Canal in the sediment." Before the Industrial Revolution, the Irwell and other rivers which now flow into the Manchester Ship Canal were trout rivers. Fish restocking in 1988-89 introduced 12,000 coarse fish to the Quays, with high growth rates subsequently recorded for such species as roach, perch and carp. Later, in 1993, the trout would also be returned.

Fish spawning was supported by placing artificial reefs and submerged plants in the basins. The locals who once turned their noses up at the terrible smell of the docks began to fish there. Floating baskets were strategically placed to entice wild birds. With clean water and a thriving acquatic ecosystem, the scene was set for a range of water sports to come to the Quays.

Within a few years, its once-polluted waters would be hosting the unthinkable - a university boat race between Manchester and Salford.

Development Plan review

Salford's commitment to water quality was an important factor in changing perceptions about the Quays. By the late 1980s, the redevelopment of London's Docklands with its waterfront "yuppie" housing and smart office districts was already having an effect on how rundown urban docks should be valued. The British economy was booming in the South-East and this recovery was beginning to reach other parts of the country, including Manchester. Amid a buoyant market for office development which was threatening to push the mixed-use strategy at Salford Quays out of kilter, Tony Struthers and his team recognised that the Development Plan needed to be reviewed and rolled forward. In particular, better public transport access was needed to maximise development opportunities on the Quays and reduce the environmental impact of commuter traffic. Planning for an extension of the Manchester Metrolink light tram system to run through the area became essential.

The Development Strategy Review was published in August 1988. Again this was a collaborative effort between Struthers's department and Shepheard Epstein Hunter. It sought to uphold the planning principles and visual character of the original plan but, significantly, it introduced a new element that, during the next decade, would lead directly to the building of The Lowry. The Introduction to the Review reflected the progress that had been made in just three years:

"Salford Quays is now well established as an example of how a derelict inner-city site can be imaginatively transformed into a new living and working community." No longer did Roger Rees and Tony Struthers warn of the potential for devastation, as in 1985, but warmed to the potential of the Quays to become "a major visitor attraction in the North of England. Its unique waterfront will be complemented by equally impressive attractions on land."

As commercial development threatened to encroach on all available land on the redeveloped site, it was important to preserve some key leisure amenities for the public. The Review was explicit, describing a "water fun centre" and the "Salford Quays Centre for the Performing Arts". For the first time, the forerunner to The Lowry was written down in black and white. Its precise details, which included a 2,500-seat main auditorium, music library and multi-storey car park, would later change (not least with the vital inclusion of galleries to house Salford's L S Lowry collection), but its location on the tip of Pier 8 facing Trafford Wharfside was spot-on. Nobody knows exactly who originated the idea. Tony Struthers remembers "a consensus of the team" opting for performing arts and watersports facilities to be included in the Review, "the former in response to the Hallé looking for a new home and as a fanciful gesture in the spirit of the Sydney Opera House, the latter in recognition of all the work done on water quality".

Royal Salford Hall

The Development Strategy Review of 1988 reflected the more upbeat and ambitious mood which was around Salford Quays at the time. One aspect of the document in particular caught Peter Hunter's imagination: Salford Quays Centre for the Performing Arts. In his gently inquiring way, he kept turning the idea over and over in his mind. More and more, he began to visualise this arts showcase as the anchor for the entire regeneration of the site. The following year, to advance

his ideas, Hunter created a sketch in which the Royal Albert Hall was superimposed onto the site, its domed form tucked neatly into the finger of the pier. The actual artwork was drawn by Gerald Brady at Shepheard Epstein Hunter.

"What I was trying to show was a popular place for people to go to on the Quays, a non-élitist arts venue hosting everything from Pavarotti to variety shows and boxing, like the Royal Albert Hall," said Hunter. "I called it the Royal Salford Hall." Within weeks, his fantasy was being discussed with great animation by all the key players in the project. In a single sketch, he had created the vision for The Lowry; he had turned an idea into a realisable objective that would, from that moment on, be pursued with great tenacity and imagination.

2 THE PROJECT TAKES SHAPE

"How many have bemoaned the lack of vision in this country, have said that the *grands projets* adorning France could never happen here? The Millennium Commission is your opportunity to create our own great landmark...."

Rt Hon Peter Brooke, MP, Chairman of the Millennium Commission

Peter Hunter's sketch of the "Royal Salford Hall" hangs today in the committee corridor of Salford City Council. Back in 1989 it prompted serious discussion on how such an ambitious facility for concerts, opera, ballet and drama could be incorporated into Salford Quays. "I intended it to be a catalyst and so it proved," said Hunter. "People find it hard to understand size and scale. By placing the Royal Albert Hall, which seats 7,000 people, on the dock, I showed what could be achieved. The Victorians were so clever at fitting a lot of people into a confined space. You could easily fit the Royal Albert Hall into a large, leafy surburban garden but if I said you could fit 7,000 people into a back garden, nobody would believe me."

Hunter's vision was initially rebuffed by Salford's engineer Roger Hindle, who said that the planning authorities would never allow 7,000 people to congregate in a single complex on the Quays. "That was a blow for me," said Hunter. But the exercise nevertheless focused everyone's mind. It is interesting to note how so many highly numerate and literate local government officers, accountants, bureaucrats and business people were able to make the mental leap, not as a result of a footnoted report full of bar charts but in response to one simple piece of visual communication. Sometimes a picture really is worth a thousand words. According to Salford planner Tony Struthers, "It gave us the concept. Now we had to find ways to bring it about."

John Willis, who was in charge of finance at Salford at the time, explained: "The drawing inspired the imagination. We'd got so far with the development of the Quays and we were looking at ways to make it different. This provided the germ of an idea. If we could fit the Albert Hall on the Quays, then what were our options? Back then, our only funding options were the old Urban Programme as the Lottery had not been invented. So it was very much an act of faith. The Council committed itself to seeing how far it could go and what it could achieve, and with Roger Rees as chief executive, we just started to develop it from there in an opportunistic way."

Revealing the streak of pragmatism and steel which characterised Salford's approach in developing The Lowry as a project, Willis said: "Peter Hunter's sketch gave a sense of a grand design, and of capacity. But first and foremost, I was thinking, how does this relate to the people of Salford and what will they get out of it?" Bill Hinds, who had become leader of the Council in 1988, was of a similar mind: "I always had strong views about what the development could bring to Salford, namely employment, much-needed investment, putting the city on the map. That was very important."

When BBC journalist Felicity Goodey returned from Italy to the North-West of England in 1989, she received news of "that sketch" and the interest it was generating. "I thought, here we go again, this will be a rollercoaster ride for Salford," said Goodey. "But I really wanted them to succeed. You could see their officers weren't in it for medals or self-aggrandisement. They were only interested in helping people and they deserved some help themselves."

Reserving the space

Ironically, as the British economy turned from boom to bust in the early 1990s, the property recession rode to the project's aid. The slowdown in take-up of office space revealed over-capacity of commercial development and enabled the City Council to make a strong case for reserving the prime site of Pier 8 at Salford Quays for a public amenity building with adjacent open space. As Britain was gripped by a new economic downturn, land for commercial development was no longer at a premium and the idea of a cultural centre was allowed to take shape without the pressures on use it might otherwise have faced. "Up to that point it was just noisy enthusiasts like myself saying, wouldn't it be lovely!" said Peter Hunter. "Now a whole formal process of developing the idea began."

This process involved a series of seminars and brainstorming sessions led by Salford City Council. Financial issues were studied by UBS Phillips and Drew, architectural ones by Shepheard Epstein Hunter; consultations with the arts community produced a more detailed brief. Meanwhile Hunter resigned as a partner from Shepheard Epstein Hunter, started his own practice and became "an adviser and friend" to the project. Economic and planning consultants Pieda carried out the first feasibility study on the Pier 8 scheme. And, importantly, the idea of incorporating the works of L S Lowry (1887-1976) into special galleries within the building was discussed for the first time. Salford's most famous artist was well represented by a collection held by Salford City Council. "Strategically, we had some important assets," recalled John Willis. "We had the finest collection of Lowrys which were tucked away in a corner and, in my opinion, deserved a bigger stage. We started to think how we could exploit the Lowrys and the cultural heritage of the city - if we didn't use them, we were missing a trick. But all the time the idea was to see how this could lead to economic regeneration and create employment."

With the concept now encompassing visual as well as performing arts, Salford published a brochure in 1990 to promote the scheme. It was called "The Salford Centre" (Peter Hunter's cherished Royal Salford Hall having been dropped) and its attractions included theatre, opera, music, performance, galleries, art and heritage. Its educational uses were highlighted, as were its European credentials. The gleaming high-quality infrastructure of Salford Quays, with new homes, shops, hotels and leisure facilities being built, was portrayed as the vibrant setting for this cultural jewel. The brochure was, however, speculative in that it did not make any attempt to describe the precise form the building might take.

Architectural appointment

That was the subject of intense debate as Peter Hunter pressed for an architectural competition to be held to appoint "a top European architect" to carry out the commission. In this he was supported by Janet Roberts, a member of Tony Struthers's team who had worked on the Salford Quays development since 1986. Roberts, a town planner by training, became coordinator of The Salford Centre in 1989 and worked with Pieda on the feasibility study. "We saw it as very important to build on the quality of the urban design, to make a serious statement about it," said Roberts. "So we needed to search for an architect of international repute with masterplanning experience to create a plan for the Pier 8 site."

Armed with advice from the Royal Institute of British Architects, Roberts wrote to 35 different European practices inviting expressions of interest in the scheme. The replies were assessed by the project's steering group, which at that time comprised representatives from the City Council, the project's consulting engineers Ove Arup and Pieda, as well as Peter Hunter. A shortlist of four was drawn up. Two were British architects (James Stirling Michael Wilford & Associates and Arup Associates) and two were Spanish (Ricardo Bofill and Garcia Parades). These firms were invited to visit the Salford Quays site. Janet Roberts and Roger Hindle, Salford's head of engineering, subsequently visited European cities to inspect their built works and interview their previous clients. After much soul-searching, Salford reached its decision. In 1991, the practice of Stirling and Wilford was appointed as masterplanner for the site. James Stirling, the son of a Liverpool ship's engineer, and Michael Wilford were the impressive architects of a number of high-profile schemes including the Staatsgalerie in Stuttgart and Number One The Poultry in the City of London. Janet Roberts admitted that

Michael Wilford at work in his office, Fitzroy Square, London, July 1998.

the Staatsgalerie in Stuttgart was a defining factor in the decision. "It was so intriguing, such a lovely building, and Stuttgart has some similarities to Manchester in that it is primarily seen as a commercial centre and not a cultural centre. We looked at studies of the project and the Staatsgalerie did succeed in creating economic improvements and raising the profile of the city, in the way we want The Lowry to do for Salford."

The Staatsgalerie project was so distinctive that, unusually, it passed into popular culture when it starred in a Rover TV commercial in which two Germans drive a Rover through Stuttgart and arrive at the building. "Britischer Architekt," they say admiringly, making the point that the British can design well too. But Peter Hunter was not so sure that the Staatsgalerie alone swayed the selectors: "It wasn't just Stuttgart. Jim Stirling warmed to the project. He got on with the people at Salford. He spent time and walked around the site. Initially he thought it wasn't going to happen and I tried hard to convince him that it would. He moved the position of the building and pushed it into a corner of the pier because he said he'd never designed a building with so much space around it before."

Early sketch ideas

Hunter was excited by how the scheme was being developed: "I loved the first sketches by Jim Stirling. All that geometric complexity and excitement. It looked like a large ship steaming into the docks." He also recalled that at the first presentation of Stirling Wilford's ideas on the masterplan, Salford's chief executive Roger Rees looked at the massing of the proposed building and exclaimed: "It looks like Heysham Power Station." To which James Stirling replied dryly: "Well, you've got the scale then."

According to Michael Wilford, "Right at the outset there was a sense of the chemistry that might develop between the parties involved." The masterplan demonstrated how the Pier 8 site might be developed, showing an "opera house" in relation to a public plaza, hotel, car park and a future commercial development. *Guardian* architectural critic Deyan Sudjic reviewed the plan favourably. Although he described Salford Quays as "a location as plausible as the middle of the Sahara desert" (old metropolitan prejudices evidently died hard despite the strenuous improvements to the docks), he praised the project as "a rediscovery by a local authority of serious architecture" and for making "no apologies for cutting across so many conventional expectations". Looked at today, Stirling and Wilford's first thoughts on The Lowry are elegant and powerful, capturing a spirit for the project that would later be effectively developed through design and construction.

But before Stirling Wilford could build on the positive early reaction, the practice was shaken to the core by Sir James Stirling's sudden and unexpected death. On 25 June 1992, the day ironically

scheduled for a presentation by the architects to The Salford Centre project group, Stirling died suddenly in hospital following a routine operation that went tragically wrong. He was 68 and had been given a knighthood on his last day at work before going into hospital. According to his biographer Mark Girouard, Stirling was "cut off at the height of his powers". His physical and creative presence at the heart of the Stirling Wilford practice had been immense, and in the immediate aftermath of his death his partner Michael Wilford was left holding the ring. At Salford City Council, there were deep misgivings about what would happen. "When Jim Stirling died, we did wonder if the practice would be able to handle it," said Tony Struthers.

At a sensitive and critical time, however, Wilford, rose to the challenge. After all, he had worked with Stirling for 32 years, 21 of those as his partner. Stirling's

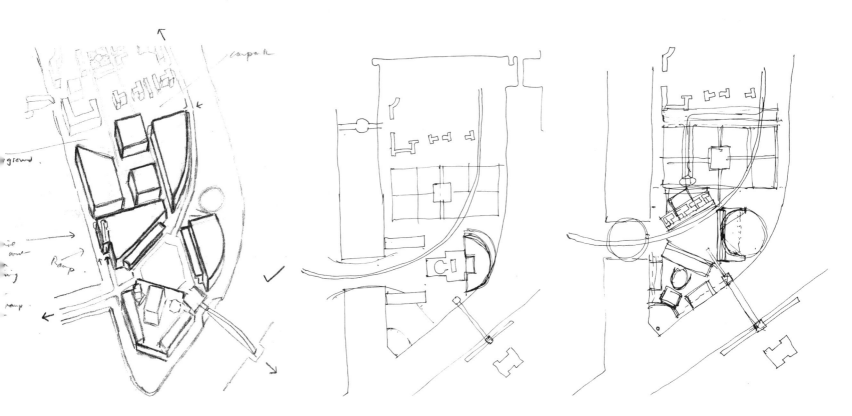

final comments and notes on the project were incorporated into a full presentation which two members of the team took to Salford on 25 June. The next month, in July, Michael Wilford successfully presented the masterplan to a meeting of arts and media organisations (from the BBC to Rambert Dance) invited to Salford to give feedback and express support. More than 100 representatives of local, national and regional companies turned up. According to Janet Roberts, "The response of these organisations was so positive and helpful that we were given the confidence to really push on with the project. That led to a new round of work."

Enlarging the project

A new Europe-wide tendering process to appoint consultants to the scheme was set in train, and in June the following year Salford City Council voted formally to proceed. "It was on a wing and a prayer because at the time there was no way to fund it," recalled Struthers. With Stirling Wilford, later to become Michael Wilford & Partners, confirmed as architects of The Salford Centre building, the architectural brief needed to be proven and developed in the form of a feasibility study. In August 1993, Theatre Projects Consultants, an international team of theatre designers, arts managers and technicians, was invited to undertake this work. According to Theatre Projects director Jeremy Godden, "Initially we were incredulous that such an elaborate building costing huge sums of money should be planned for the middle of nowhere. But we began to see that with the right team, the right management and the right approach it could work."

Theatre Projects had been founded in 1967 by Richard Pilbrow, Sir Laurence Olivier's lighting designer at the Old Vic and a key technical player in the building of the National Theatre on London's South Bank. Its experience of the workings of theatre buildings was extensive, and its reading of the relationship between space, architecture and audience in many ways unique.

First sketches for the schemes by (left) James Stirling and (centre and right) Michael Wilford. A precise geometric approach was evident from the start.

Decisions on theatre capacity were already some way down the line, and the subject of constant debate and revision, but when Theatre Projects produced its Salford Centre feasibility study in January 1994, its authors David Staples and Lou Fleming made two key recommendations. First, they suggested that the capacity of the main Lyric Theatre should be enlarged to 1,650 seats (it was originally set at 1,200 seats in Stirling Wilford's 1992 scheme); second, they focused support on the idea of a second, adaptable auditorium, which had also been incorporated into the 1992 Stirling Wilford plan, on the grounds that its ability to offer thrust-stage, end-stage and theatre-in-the-round configurations would make it ideal for community theatre.

Just as the proposed theatre space of The Salford Centre was studied by experts to determine its feasibility, so was the gallery space. Theatre Projects brought a Canadian consultancy called Lord Cultural Resources onto the project team to advise Salford City Council on the spatial and environmental conditions that would be required to successfully house and display its valuable collection of paintings and drawings by L S Lowry. Lord is an international museum planning firm, which has been active in the UK since the mid-1980s. Set up in Toronto in 1981 by husband-and-wife team Barry and Gail Dexter Lord, it has published a standard text on museum planning and management.

Through a process of research, Lord Cultural Resources reached the conclusion that the visual art dimension of the project needed to be reconsidered. Not only did the mainly small-scale works in the L S Lowry collection require an intimate sequence of custom-made galleries but there needed to be a study centre for the collection. In addition, having studied the social demographics of the North-West of England, which has the highest concentration of children under 15 in the whole of Europe, Lord proposed a second gallery attraction - an interactive gallery for children and families which explored the nature of the performing and visual arts. The original plan specified only a single L S Lowry gallery, little more than an enhanced lobby presence, but gradually over time a new, more complex picture emerged as a result of discussions and consultations with different galleries. A trio of elements - a sequence of Lowry galleries, a Lowry study centre and a children's gallery - were advocated for the building.

Michael Wilford found himself designing a scheme that was growing rapidly with every meeting of the Salford Centre project group and each new consultant's report. "From our first sketch design to the concept design, the building virtually doubled in size, with the inclusion of the smaller adaptable theatre and the new children's gallery," he explained. "All the support facilities, from dressing rooms to storage, also needed to get bigger." Nobody doubted that the project was enriched as well as enlarged by new expert input, but Wilford pointed out that "all of this made a dramatic difference to the scale and density of the building." In retrospect one can see how difficult this was for Wilford to manage as the custodian of a singular architectural vision for the project. The outsider's view of the architect-designed arts centre is usually of a form or construct dictated by a single author, a moment of architectural perfection frozen in time. But Wilford and his team found themselves boarding a moving train which placed continual demands on their ability to improvise and be flexible.

Lottery to the rescue

While the feasibility studies and consultations helped to give the project shape, they did little to make The Lowry Centre Salford, as it came to be named, stack up in terms of funding. John Willis and his colleagues knew the Urban Programme was being phased out as a source of finance. The picture, briefly, looked hopeless. Then Salford got the break its determination and sense of decency deserved. The National Lottery came on the scene - a development destined to

Top: Jeremy Godden of Theatre Projects: "Initially we were incredulous."

Above: Button badge for supporters of the project.

Hayes Davidson computer illustration of The Lowry's left flank overlooking the Manchester Ship Canal, based on Wilford's early concept design. The purple cladding and massive screen above the canopy would later change during development.

transform the future of Salford's national arts centre scheme as well as many other cherished local authority projects. "We knew we couldn't use Lottery money directly for new industry," said Willis, who became chief executive in 1993 just as the Lottery was first being discussed. "But what we could do was create jobs and wealth indirectly. We thought we had a good scheme which would make a big impact, so we decided to run with it and see what happened."

Bidding for Lottery money quickened the pace and changed the complexion of the project. But importantly, a lot of the groundwork had already been done by Salford. A plan existed, consultants were in place and a consultation process firmly established. Within the City Council, planner Janet Roberts and deputy treasurer Eric Lamprell began, in October 1994, to coordinate the Lottery bid and marshall the programme to make it happen. Lamprell, a key figure at this stage, recalled being invited to participate: "John Willis stressed it was only a small job and asked to borrow me just for 'a couple of weeks'." What followed was one of the most difficult funding hurdles ever cleared by a local authority pursuing an arts project. "The actual process of securing funding was probably the single most stimulating process I've been involved in," observed Willis. "It was immensely complicated, requiring an immense amount of determination by a vast army of people. It was blood, sweat and tears all the way."

Project champion

The Lowry Centre project badly needed a champion. As Salford was in the process of setting up a steering group to make the Lottery bid on the arm's-length principle, the name of BBC journalist Felicity Goodey came back into the frame. "Tony Struthers called me in summer 1994 and explained how the project was getting bigger," recalled Goodey. "He told me about the Lottery bid and the steering group and said he wanted me to chair it. I asked how much time it would take and he said it would be four meetings a year. It later became four meetings a week!" John Willis was in no doubt that Goodey would give the project the lift it needed. "Felicity enjoyed local credibility. She had been reporting on the gloom and doom in the area for years and had always

delved below the surface. She brought a magnetic personality, although at the time we didn't appreciate fully the capacity and commitment she would bring."

The first meeting of the Lowry Centre steering group, with Felicity Goodey in the chair, was held on 6 October 1994. Other steering group members included Peter Hunter, John Willis, Bill Hinds (Salford City Council leader) and Michael Unger (Editor of the *Manchester Evening News*) - see page 176. Secretary to the steering group was Christopher Hulme, an executive assistant in John Willis's office, who recalled: "Trying to convince someone like Michael Unger that the blackspot of Salford Quays could have a national arts centre with a public plaza and Metrolink to the centre of Manchester was a real test of credibility. But Felicity was an excellent communicator who could always take people with her."

The minutes of that historic first meeting were interspersed with quotations from a speech given by Millennium Commission chairman Peter Brooke, MP, in which he outlined the broad millennial criteria which defined use of Lottery funds. "How many have bemoaned the lack of vision in this country, have said that the *grands projets* adorning France could never happen here? The Millennium Commission is your opportunity to create our own great landmark," he said. As if that were not spur enough to the steering group, he declared: "Lift your eyes from the familiar, the mediocre, the mundane and look to the glory of the nation."

Consulting the community

Christopher Hulme, who would later be seconded from Salford City Council to The Lowry Centre Trust and its subsidiary companies in the key role of company secretary to play an essential part in the realisation of the Lowry, recognised the importance of local consultation. Out of context, grandiose plans for an "opera house" sounded incongruous to the local Salford community. "When we started the Lowry project, we already had a community strategy and mechanism to engage local people in decision-making," said Hulme. "Our consultative methods had even been piloted in a ward adjacent to Salford Quays." This was to become more important as the scheme progressed. Indeed, one of Peter Brooke's statements made it imperative to involve the local community: "If the projects which we are to support are to stand the test of time, they must be of and for the man and woman in the street."

Felicity Goodey remembered spending a day with the tenants' association on a local estate. "They cross-examined us fiercely," she recalled. "But then one lady came up and said: 'I may be poor but I don't want my children to be poor. This could be a great opportunity for their future.' As we informed people, there was a commonsense approach to the project. Many local councillors were sceptical so we always tried to give them the whole picture."

While Salford City Council prepared the ground locally, it also launched a charm offensive to win hearts and minds nationally. As John Willis said: "When I enter something, I enter to win." MPs in the region were lobbied for support. Five famous artistic sons of Salford - Albert Finney, Sir Peter Maxwell Davies, Harold Riley, Ben Kingsley and Robert Powell - were invited to become founder patrons of the project. At a London reception for The Lowry, held at the Royal Academy, Councillor Bill Hinds made an impassioned speech about the social importance of the project which won a round of applause from normally cynical metropolitan journalists.

Project champion Felicity Goodey with Bill Alexander of the Millennium Commission.

"Art in this country has always been a class issue. I've always felt that ordinary working-class people, kids especially, have never really been encouraged to participate in art," he said later. "I don't expect everyone will suddenly become an opera lover or a ballet lover or an expert on painting, but I do believe that everyone should have the opportunity to develop their minds and not feel it's not for the likes of them, but for somebody higher up the social strata."

In April 1995, the *Manchester Evening News* conducted a readers' poll about expenditure on The Lowry in which two-thirds of the respondents supported the development. "Considering the problems that many people in the city faced, that was remarkable. I was proud of that," remarked Hinds, whose willingness to take a huge political gamble over the project showed courage and leadership.

Complex funding matrix

The Lowry Centre steering group met on a monthly basis to try to shape up the Lottery bid. Having invested heavily in consultants and feasibility studies, Salford was gambling on winning, but even at an early stage John Willis recognised that the bid would need to be resilient to overcome setbacks: "As we got into the complications of the Lottery, it became obvious that the rules wouldn't allow our project to be funded by the Millennium Commission alone, so we had to split the project up and decide which elements fell into the remit of the Arts Council or the National Heritage Memorial Fund or the Millennium Commission. But the rules didn't allow for different funders to come together to jointly fund a single project. To get anywhere we had to break the mould and convince people."

The issue was further complicated by a new development in the project - the inclusion in the bid of a "National Industrial Virtual Reality Centre" as part of The Lowry's arts showcase. This came about following a lunch between John Willis and the Pro-Vice Chancellor of Salford University, Professor Peter Brandon, at which Willis was briefed on the university's world-leading research in the emerging field of virtual reality. In opportunistic mode, Willis immediately saw a way to link this local technological pre-eminence to the Lowry bid. Virtual reality was future-oriented and millennial in spirit. Within the Lowry project, it could be an educational component introducing the digital arts alongside the performing and visual arts. A subsequent presentation by Brandon and his Salford University virtual reality team to The Lowry Centre steering group settled matters. A virtual reality centre accommodating the Salford University research team in its own building next to the Lowry was written into the Lottery bid. "In truth, we thought it would fall off the edge of the bid, but it didn't," said Goodey. "In fact it became an important element in the total concept."

By this point, so complicated were the financing criteria that despite taking exhaustive soundings from the various funding bodies, a deal stubbornly refused to fall into place. The Arts Council, for example, could only fund living artists, and not artists who were dead such as L S Lowry. The Lowry concept was so multi-faceted that arguments raged over whether it was an arts or heritage project. The industrial applications of the virtual reality centre (an element later to be a source of considerable debate and subject to radical revision) muddied the waters further.

Then there was the whole issue of matching funding because the Lottery grant would not shoulder the whole cost - and the relationship to consider between the commercial and subsidised elements of the project. From the outset, The Lowry Centre steering group did not want to build a centre that relied on large subsidies well into the 21st century. "The bid kept falling between several stools," said Felicity Goodey. "We had bad days. On one occasion Sir John Hall led a trio of Millennium Commissioners up to Salford and explained that they couldn't fund anything which was a commercial scheme. But how were we to get in matching private money? We were on the floor."

Opposite: The plan of
The Lowry Centre was
painted in different colours
on the Pier 8 site and
photographed from the air as
part of the Lottery bid.

Below: Doug Weston,
Millennium Commission
director of projects,
pictured at Salford Quays,
November 1997:
"It was a unique
scheme for the area."

A deal is struck

Progress was agonisingly slow but with the help of Sir John Hall and Jennie Page, chief executive of the Millennium Commission, a deal was eventually brokered. In an unprecedented move, Page was instrumental in getting all the funding bodies together around a table to co-fund the project. The Arts Council would fund the theatres; the National Heritage Memorial Fund would support the L S Lowry galleries and study centre; the Millennium Commission would be responsible for funding the children's gallery and the virtual reality centre as well as foyers, car parking, the plaza, the footbridge to Trafford Park Wharfside and other general works.

In a triumph of negotiation, a funding package of £64.3 million was agreed, as the Millennium Commission earmarked The Lowry Centre to become one of its flagship projects. According to Millennium Commission director of projects Doug Weston, the funding matrix which emerged was "natural and obvious - this was an arts complex with theatres and a heritage centre showing the Lowry pictures. The Millennium Commission provided the glue to cement these two components together." Weston was in no doubt as to the project's special attributes: "It was a unique scheme for the area. The use of the canalside was interesting to us, as was the regeneration potential. We saw it as a catalytic project to spur others to invest in the area. The water cleaning had already provided some environmental benefit."

This was a view shared by Arts Council Dance Panel chairman Prue Skene. "It was very much a landmark project," said Skene, who was later appointed chairman of the Arts Council's Lottery Panel, "because of the joint promotion of theatres and an art gallery under one roof, the siting in the landscape, and the regeneration - bringing a whole area back to life." With projections in the mid-1990s estimating the total worth of the entire project, including an adjacent commercial development, to be £127 million, matching funds were obtained from English Partnerships (£5.1 million) and the European Regional Development Fund (£15.1 million), alongside Salford City Council's contribution (to the value of £3.2 million). Sources of private sector funding were identified, and Trafford Park Development Corporation and the University of Salford also joined the funders.

It became clear that the architecture of The Lowry, with its artistic amalgam of identifiable and separate component parts, was instrumental in the successful assembly of the funding package. Chairman of the Arts Council, Lord Gowrie, in likening the modular building to "a Dan Dare spaceship", had promised architect Michael Wilford that he would challenge other funding bodies to take on different parts of the project. And so it proved. In the run-up to the submission of the bid, Salford kept up the pressure, seeking political support wherever it could be found. "We had a remarkable occasion towards the end of the bidding process when the then Deputy Prime Minister Michael Heseltine, a member of the Millennium Commission, visited the site to interview us," recalled John Willis. "He then rang the local BBC TV station. Although he couldn't commit at the time, the fact that he went on the local news to talk about the Lowry Centre spoke volumes."

Assessing the bid

The three main funders, the Millennium Commission, Arts Council and National Heritage Memorial Fund, needed to assess the project. Their choice of assessor was Henry Wrong, the vastly experienced former administrator of the Barbican Arts Centre in London, who was well known to the chairmen of all three organisations. On 1 September 1995, following interviews with more than 20 people close to the project, Wrong announced his findings in a succinct report to Jeremy Newton, National Lottery director at the Arts Council of England.

"The Lowry Centre is very much a project for the people rather than a monument to civic pride," he declared, stating that there was no large-scale arts centre in the region and that a number of major touring companies had expressed their dissatisfaction with performing arts facilities in Manchester. He explained that the theatres would not be viable on their own (if the visual art component was removed) without a costly redesign by Michael Wilford & Partners; and in any case, the City Council would be reluctant to support a project in which the L S Lowry galleries were not a principal element. But he added: "There is a leap of faith required to give the go-ahead for the Centre to be built." His chief recommendation was that a proper business plan be prepared for the first five years of operation relating running costs to artistic policy.

"I told the Arts Council that before they could take the project seriously, it needed a proper business plan," recalled Henry Wrong. "The Lowry faced a very rough ride against a fair amount of organised opposition in Manchester. So it really needed to be worked out." Salford City Council asked Wrong who should carry out this task and he in turn consulted with impresario Raymond Gubbay to find the right person for the job - someone who could match the City Council's expertise in bidding for capital funding with operational expertise in running a national arts venue. Gubbay proposed Stephen Hetherington of Hetherington Seelig, a management company with a proven track record in planning international arts festivals and presenting major arts events worldwide. Hetherington was a former classical musician who had forged a successful career on the business side of the arts, a clear-headed thinker who acted as a consultant to governments and cultural institutions globally. Hetherington possessed strong commercial instincts and a distinct management methodology which had worked in a range of different contexts. His curriculum vitae contained a breadth of experience from corporate planning and capital projects to community-based arts activities. The Lowry would demand these characteristics in large measure in the development of an over-arching philosophical, structural and operational business plan.

Honing the plan

Stephen Hetherington's powerful vision for the project, and total commitment in realising it, would become one of the most telling factors in the making of The Lowry. Over the next five years he would bring the project into being as its chief executive. On a number of international

arts construction projects which have an urban regeneration focus, the presence of a strong, single-minded leader to drive things through has been a major factor in success. One thinks, for instance, of the direct impact of the Tokyo mayor Shunichi Suzuki on the building of the Tokyo International Forum, designed by Rafael Vignoly. Hetherington was destined to fill this thrusting role at The Lowry, but his position extended beyond that to encompass the detailed work of the senior manager who orchestrates a range of technical and creative inputs, deliberating and presiding over an entire spectrum of interlocking design decisions relating to site, business plan, building and programme.

However, this web of processes woven by Hetherington would be for later. At the outset his role was strictly as a consultant on a short-term contract. "Henry Wrong clearly saw that the Salford plan lacked focus," said Hetherington. "It needed to be rationalised - and quickly." The Lowry had to submit the Lottery application by early January 1996. Hetherington found himself after a busy autumn working solidly through the Christmas holidays - a memory that sticks with him is that of his three-year-old daughter trying to lure him out of his study and away from his desk with a piece of Christmas cake.

Stephen Hetherington, a clear thinker on the business side of the arts, was destined to lead the project.

Below: Matt cartoon
that appeared in the
Daily Telegraph on the day
Salford City Council was
awarded £64 million from the
Lottery for The Lowry Centre.

Bottom: John Willis, Salford
City Council chief executive,
who was "kicked out"of
the Savoy Hotel at the
moment of triumph.

MATT

'There are those ghastly
people who got £64m
from the Lottery'

Following Hetherington's rapid work over the holiday season, in which ideas were sharpened and the complex funding matrix teased into shape, The Lowry Centre's National Lottery bid was ready. It was duly submitted on time in a summary document boldly phrased in the language of "cultural renaissance" and "regional competitiveness" that was part of the political argot of the mid-1990s. The project was heralded as creating 6,500 jobs over the next ten years, regenerating 56 acres of derelict land, attracting more than 2.5 million visitors each year, and generating more than £100 million in private investment. It had grown enormously in scale and ambition. The famous sons of Salford weighed in. "The idea of having a concert hall at the end of the street where you were born is almost too much. What a wonderful idea!" declared Sir Peter Maxwell Davies in the bid document. Although The Lowry Centre encompassed much more than a concert hall, the sentiment was right on the button.

Now the bid work was over and all Salford City Council could do was wait. Would the scheme be given the green light, or would all their initial planning and investment be in vain? For Christopher Hulme, the decision was never in doubt: "I always thought we'd make it. I remember Councillor Bill Hinds coming into my office, shaking his head and asking, will we do it? But I thought we had a great team, very well balanced and totally committed. I felt the bid was irresistible." But if the decision went Salford's way, as the optimists on the team suggested it would, the City Council needed to handle the press announcement carefully. Both Willis and Hulme knew the mischief the media could make along the lines of "Labour council funds opera house while housing lists grow."

The gamble pays off

Working with PR consultant Staniforths, whose principal Tony Ingham had focused hard on creating a positive profile for the project in the local community, Salford devised a careful strategy for the announcement. At 9.45am on 22 February 1996, the Millennium Commission, which acted as lead funding body on the project, announced that National Lottery funding had been secured for The Lowry. Salford's great gamble had paid off. Seven years after Peter Hunter first produced his sketch of the Albert Hall on Pier 8, the development was about to enter an exciting new phase. Immediately a letter from Bill Hinds to fellow councillors and a press briefing sheet were sent out. Both communicated the same key message: "Lottery monies cannot be spent on new houses or roads, schools or social services, so our objectives remain as always - to secure jobs and economic regeneration, to raise aspiration and pride."

But if Salford chief executive John Willis felt like a pools winner that morning, his joy was cut short when he popped into the Savoy Hotel for a celebratory glass of champagne with Felicity Goodey and Janet Roberts. He wasn't wearing a tie so all three were refused entry to the restaurant. "We may have just been awarded £64 million but they still kicked us out," recalled Willis. "Our parting shot was that if the Savoy wouldn't have us, we'd just have to take tea with the Minister." The trio decamped to the office of Alistair Burt, then Minister for Manchester and Salford, to receive a friendlier welcome. Back in Salford, the announcement was followed by a celebratory dinner for council and community representatives at Pembroke Hall in March and a firework and laser show for local people at Salford Quays over the April Bank Holiday. Later that month, on 25 April 1996, The Lowry Centre Trust met for the first time - the logical conclusion of Salford City Council's commitment to hand over the project to an independent charitable trust. The Lowry Centre Trust evolved from the steering group and Felicity Goodey became its chairman.

"It was never our intention to run The Lowry," said Eric Lamprell of Salford City Council, who had worked so hard to reconcile the conflicting criteria and deadlines of so many different funders in one programme. "Our job was to promote the project, to take it to the point at which

The ground-breaking ceremony for The Lowry, on 19 June 1997, involved hundreds of local schoolchildren who had contributed to time capsules that were buried on the site.

funding was secured and a start on-site could be made. Once that happened, we put in place a partnership arrangement between the Council and the Trust. We do have representatives on the Trust but not in the majority. It's something we want to contribute to but not control."

A personal crusade

By the end of the year The Lowry Centre Trust would have a permanent chief executive to push things forward. Once hooked by the project, Stephen Hetherington allowed his candidacy to be put forward, initially with some reluctance. "Stephen is his own man and he had nearly always worked for himself. We didn't think we'd be able to persuade him to take on the full-time role," said Felicity Goodey. "But in the end I don't think he could resist the temptation to show how a world-class arts programme could be made to work without lashings of subsidy. He was also attracted, as I was, by the idea of the venue as an anchor for urban regeneration. Stephen is entrepreneurial and a hard-nosed businessman, but he also believes passionately in the power of the arts to unleash creativity in everyone. So he swapped the rich diet of his own work for an uncertain future with The Lowry."

Hetherington had some idea of what he was letting himself in for. He was acting chief executive during 1996 while interviews were conducted, and, as he explained, "I had a lot of experience of developing legal and financial models in the arts. Many of the elements of the job were familiar.

Only the scale was new. But I began to see the project as significant in my own life. It became a landmark, an opportunity to express ideas about the arts that I'd been developing for 20 years. Personally, it became too difficult to pass up."

Salford leader Bill Hinds described the Lottery anouncement as "Salford's greatest day in living memory". Lord Gowrie, then chairman of the Arts Council, described the scheme as "a magnet to attract artists and audiences from far and wide". But as Hetherington and the rest of The Lowry team basked in the brief afterglow of becoming a landmark millennium project, Jennie Page reminded them that "the hard work has only just begun". What she didn't say was just how hard it would become.

3 ARCHITECTURE IN FOCUS

"The Lowry... is not just startlingly beautiful with all its naval connotations; it is also highly functional thanks to the way its different parts are knit together, at times with what might even be described as majestic force...."

Maurizio Vogliazzo, L'Arca magazine

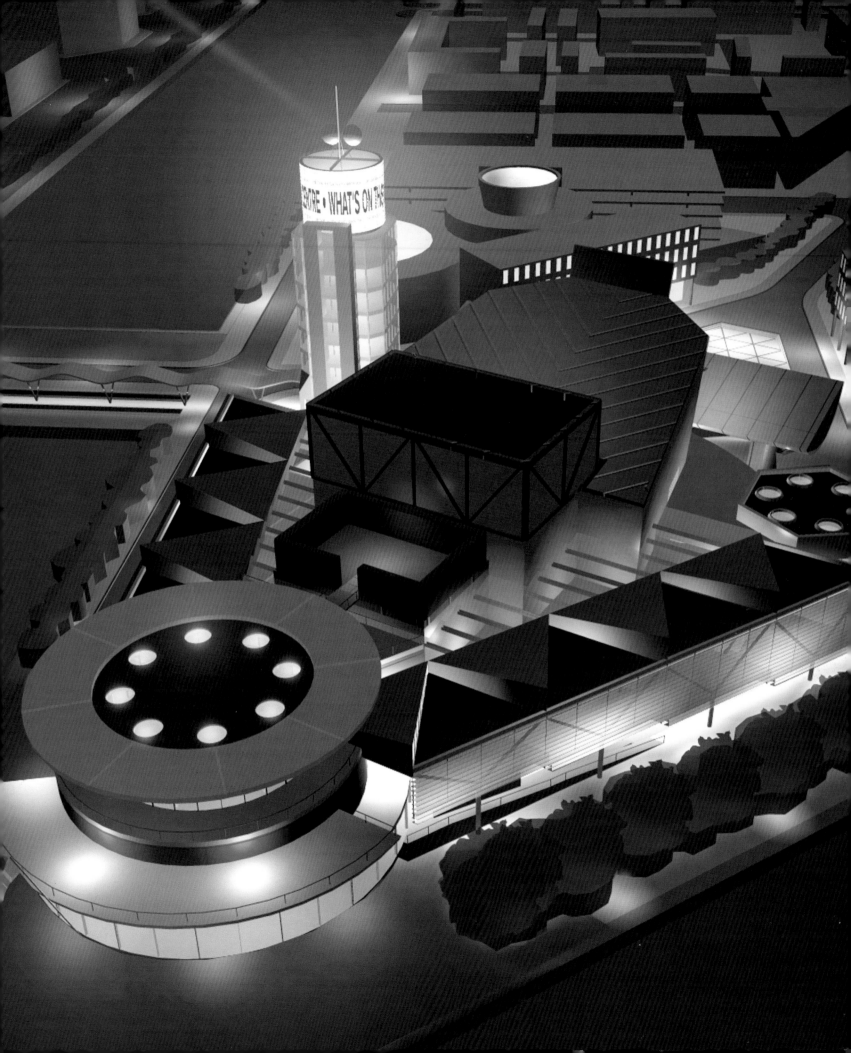

The news that The Lowry Centre would be built at Salford Quays was greeted regionally, nationally and internationally with praise both for Salford City Council's gritty belief in the project and for the imaginative quality of Michael Wilford's architectural design. While the critical reception accorded to L S Lowry himself was more mixed - national art critics debated whether his status as an artist really merited a focal role in such an expensive and significant arts showcase - there was universal admiration for what was being proposed on the triangular site at the western tip of Pier 8.

Salford had made its bold Lowry bid just as the Cardiff Bay Opera House, a spectacular new performing arts facility designed by Zaha Hadid following an international competition, was foundering in the face of local opposition, obstinacy and loss of nerve. The irony was not lost on several commentators, including Rowan Moore, editor of the influential *Blueprint* architectural magazine, who wrote in his leader: "The Lowry Centre, a project of similar scale and ambition, received staunch local authority support and received funding without a hint of controversy, even though Michael Wilford's design was no less uncompromising and unusual than Zaha Hadid's for Cardiff."

The architect himself was emphatic that "The Lowry should not be a colossal temple of culture with an imposing flight of stairs up to a giant portico." Instead, in developing the spirit of the practice's original sketches, he sought to reduce the apparent scale of the building and create a more open, inviting and accessible composition by enclosing each artistic activity within a different geometric form. The resulting collection of triangles, hexagons and circles was then arranged into a collage, glued together by a series of public foyers and promenades. "In scale and juxtaposition of elements, our approach was to compose these forms as in a sculpture," said Wilford. A large cylindrical tower, earmarked initially as an adminstration hub and designed to be seen from miles around, purposefully formed the centrepiece of the collage with smaller-scale functions providing animation around the edges. The location of The Lowry at the tip of the pier meant that all sides would be equal and exposed - there would be no back door or service yard in the scheme - and the triangular plan of the building was generated in the first instance by the geometries of road, wharf edge and link bridge across the canal.

Triangular form

This triangular plan was subsequently reinforced by three approaches to the building: the road from the entrance to Salford Quays that would address head-on the plaza in front of The Lowry; a new footbridge from Trafford Park Wharfside that would lead into the left flank of the plaza; and the new Metrolink light tram link and terminus on the adjacent Huron Basin that would

connect to the right flank of the plaza. The two theatre auditoriums - the 1,730-seat Lyric Theatre and 466-seat Quays Theatre - were arranged back to back as "blind" boxes to form the central spine of the building, which occupies 23,930 square metres of space, with views out over water and sky. As the theatres required no natural light, they could be flanked by airy public spaces and galleries. Thus, the building design took shape, with a generous foyer extending around the Lyric Theatre across the full width of the plaza frontage.

This foyer, crowned by a large canopy, provides clear visual access to all facilities and expresses the relationship between the plaza and the building's interior spaces, as well as accommodating the box office. To the left, a hexagonal pavilion signals the entrance to the Artworks Gallery, designed as a large stepped linear volume, a metal-and-glass box on the left flank of The Lowry

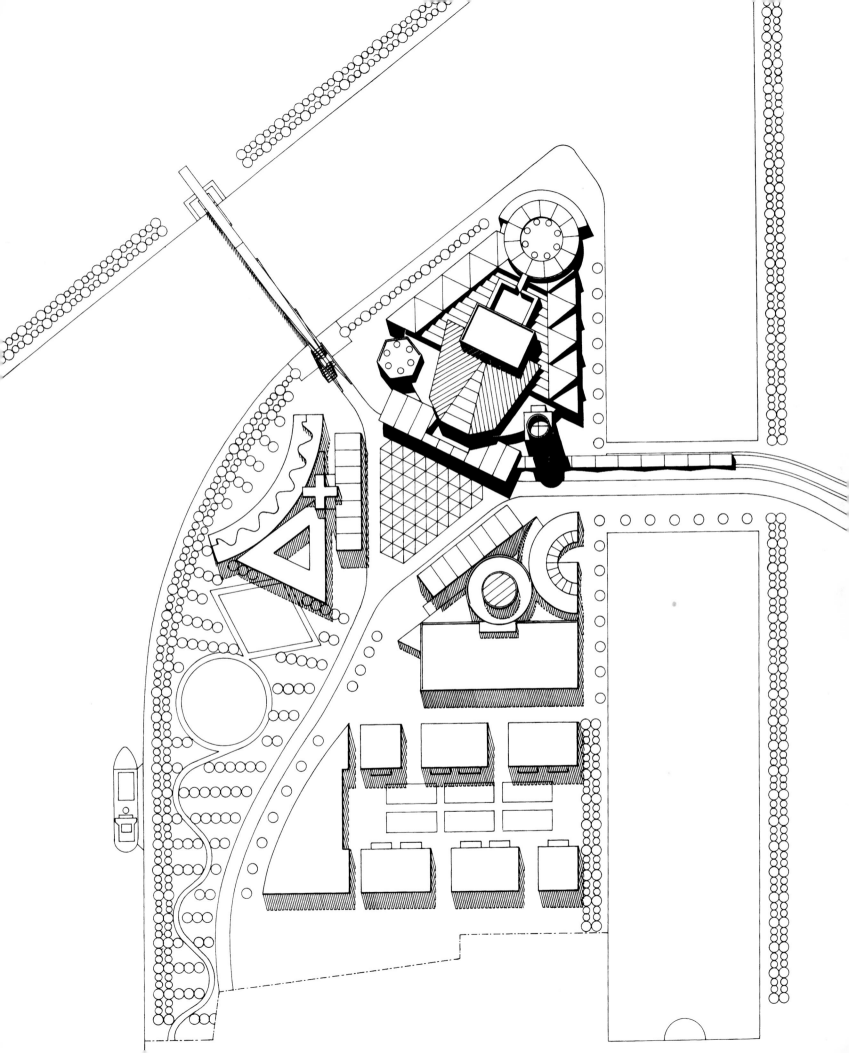

containing a series of geometric forms to accommodate audio-visual and interactive displays. To the right, escalators rise to the second-floor L S Lowry Galleries which are arranged on the right flank of The Lowry as a series of four enclosed spaces, "like diamonds in a cluster" according to Wilford.

Seating in the Lyric Theatre is arranged on three levels - stalls, dress circle and upper tier - to ensure the closest possible relationship between audience and performers, with 1,350 seats for musicals and 1,730 seats for drama. The Quays Theatre, initially known as the Adaptable Theatre because of its adaptable staging for proscenium, thrust and in-the-round performance, also has three levels but in a "courtyard" form. This smaller theatre is wrapped by a curving rear foyer at the tip of the triangular-shaped building, offering dramatic views to the west across the Manchester Ship Canal.

The two theatre foyers, front and rear, are linked by a continuous public promenade around the building which weaves together all the different activities and encloses them within a "flexible shed" of great sophistication. A ramped promenade rises to offer views into the Artworks Gallery, runs around the loggia of the building to the Lowry Galleries and returns via the escalators to the main foyer. Bar, restaurant and café facilities relate to the promenade and can be extended out to quayside terraces overlooking the canal. A Circle bar overlooking the plaza is sited above the entrance just beneath the building's impressive canopy; this serves the upper levels of the Lyric Theatre. Bars are also located in the Adaptable Theatre foyer and at the base of the tower. Movement and interaction within the building, the result of Wilford's careful composition of the different elements, will generate "an air of theatricality, festivity and anticipation", according to the architect.

A functional building

"We pride ourselves on making functional buildings," explained Wilford. "As in Stuttgart, we wanted to create a place of culture that would not intimidate, a place that would put people at their ease functionally and psychologically." He uses the analogy of an onion to describe how The Lowry is layered from the outside to the inside. This is a scheme in which the skins or layers of the building can be progressively removed to reveal what is happening inside. Each skin has its own material, colour and geometric structure. Viewed from the plaza, the first layer is the continuous glass skin to the foyer and other glazed public areas. The second layer is the purple wall on the outer concrete envelope of the Lyric Theatre which will draw people into the building. This second layer is penetrated by stairs and balconies which give direct access to all levels of the auditorium. The third layer is the yellow skin of the Lyric Theatre. (Strong colours are similarly used for the Quays Theatre - pink for the exterior walls, red for the interior.)

Top and above: Architect Michael Wilford presents his plans to The Lowry Centre Trust including Stephen Hetherington (far left) and Felicity Goodey (centre).

When Wilford first unveiled his concept design in early 1995, ahead of the Lottery bid but incorporating the recommendations of Theatre Projects and Lord Consultants filtered through the scrutiny of Stephen Hetherington and The Lowry Centre Trust, one of the most recognisable of The Lowry's skins was a daring external cladding of purple metal panels. But during design development, Wilford began to have second thoughts. "I saw the purple cladding as possibly being restrictive. I became interested in the idea of the building's exterior being able to reflect the sky and canal during the day. And at night I saw the opportunity to project light shows, light sculptures and images onto the building."

Wilford recognised that interlocking stainless steel tiles could provide a good reflection and projection surface, as well as reinforcing the nautical theme of The Lowry's design. So he agreed with the Trust to clad the building in stainless steel instead. The powerful colour theme would move inside the building, in particular to the envelopes and interiors of the theatres. The exterior would have a shimmering mirror effect, while the galleries would be designed with the appropriate white neutrality to receive both vibrant and subtle works of art.

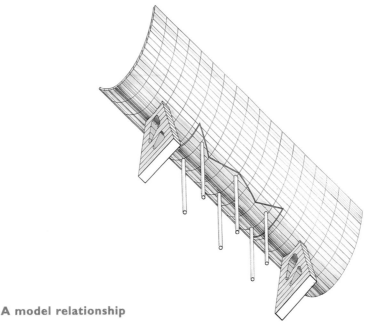

A model relationship

Michael Wilford's relationship with The Lowry Trust was as open and flexible as the building itself. Architects often have a tortuous time with their clients, fighting grimly to hang onto their original artistic vision while committees hack away at the grand design with a series of piecemeal changes. But he described the collaborative approach with the Trust as working in the best interests of his building, while being careful to give credit to Trust members for the changes and improvements they proposed. Wilford and his design team worked very closely in particular with Stephen Hetherington, John Willis and Felicity Goodey. All three he acknowledged as making a significant impact on the evolution of the building design.

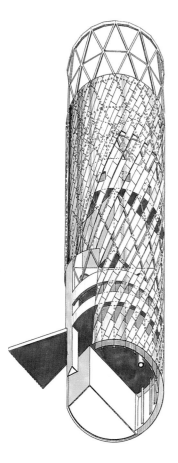

Hetherington's business plan was instrumental in defining the functional requirements of the theatres. An early Theatre Projects proposal was for a resident theatre company at The Lowry but Hetherington calculated that this would not stack up in financial terms and directed stage design requirements towards the idea of The Lowry as a "receiving house". Hetherington also questioned the wisdom of putting all administrative staff in the six-storey tower rising from the foyer. This seemed to him a remote location and could create a dangerous us-and-them stand-off between theatre and gallery staff on the one hand and support staff on the other. Hetherington's suggestion was for a "backstage village", not an ivory tower, to encourage "the sense of an artistic community". Wilford went back to the drawing board with the result that administration and theatre support areas are now grouped in a single location beneath the galleries to the north of the building. Dressing rooms for both theatres are located at stage level overlooking the quayside. As part of this arrangement, a central scene store sited between the Lyric and the Quays theatres can be reached from a truck dock accessed from the quayside.

But what would become of the tower, which the architect regarded as an essential part of his three-dimensional composition? Wilford was as determined to keep the tower as Hetherington was eager to create his backstage village. Meanwhile, Lord Cultural Resources was adamant that

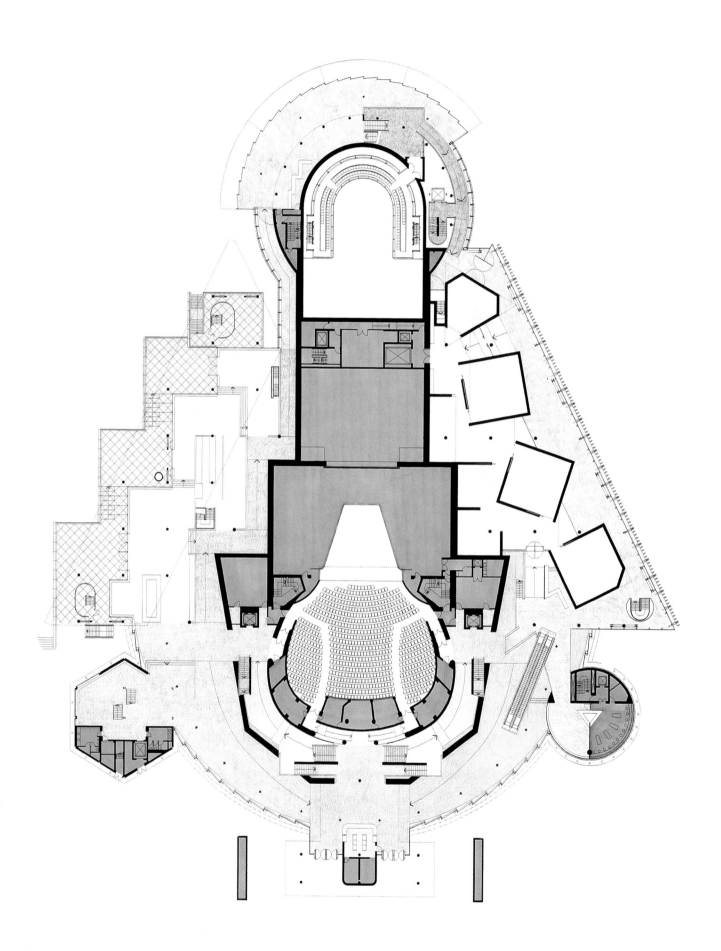

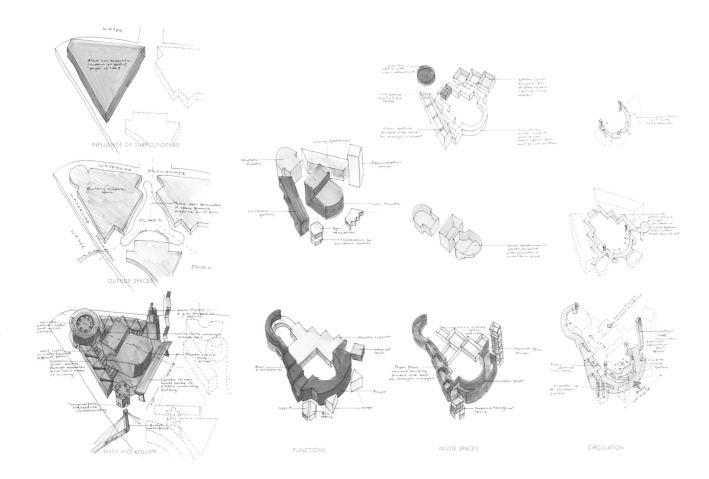

appropriate space needed to be found for a Lowry Study Centre. In seeking to trim costs, the tower could have been sacrificed from the design. But a solution was at hand: the tower was turned over for use as the study centre, complete with a triangular study room and a two-level vault to house pictures. Wilford decided to clad this element in the same perforated stainless steel as the canopy and the hexagonal pavilion, extending the idea of the layered building by creating a diaphanous skin which allows the interior forms to be glimpsed through the outer layer.

Replanning the promenade

John Willis, meanwhile, studied early plans for the all-important public promenade around the building and was concerned that the route with its ramps and bridges was largely an internal one. Willis proposed that the promenade went outside close to the water's edge at the northern tip of the building to take advantage of the canalside location. Wilford obliged with a new promenade plan. Felicity Goodey passionately expressed her view that there were never enough toilet facilities for women in arts buildings. "We responded with the most generous facilities possible located beneath the entrance," said Wilford.

Fruitful exchanges such as these followed initial misgivings, as the relationship between architect and client had got off to a bad start amid the pressures of the Lottery bid. "Salford desperately wanted visuals to enable them to solicit support for the scheme," recalled Wilford. "They demanded that we produce a virtual reality walkthrough of the building, but we explained that

Opposite: Plan showing the promenade route in blue around two levels of the scheme.

Above: Collection of geometric shapes (the architects call these 'cartoons') which build up to show the different elements of the building.

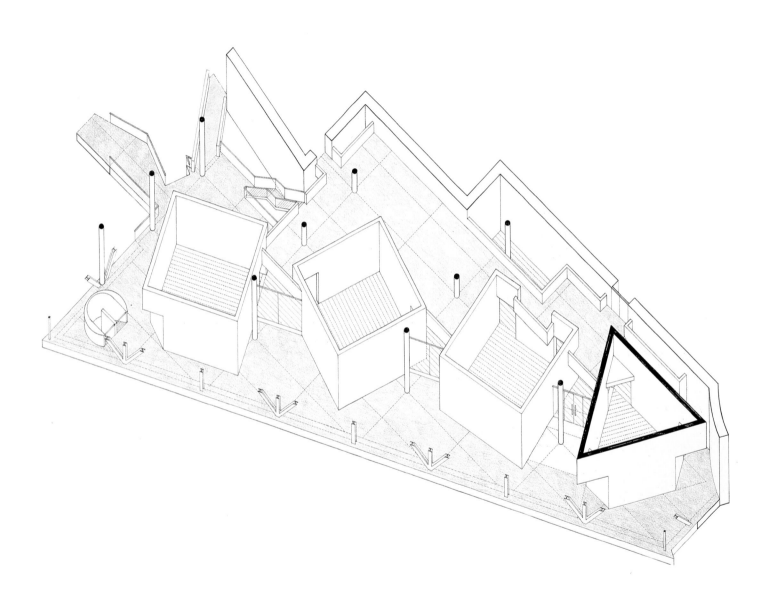

it was not possible to make computer walkthroughs with the internal aspects not designed. We said we'd develop the concept design, create an architectural model and have it photographed. Eventually they agreed and it was the model which formed the basis of the application to the funding bodies."

Wilford's stubbornness on this point was a source of considerable friction. At the City Council, private fears about architectural prima donnas were being openly voiced. Tony Struthers observed: "I think the practice was unused to the scrutiny of an English client. Perhaps they did things differently in Germany." But the further the project progressed, the more Struthers became convinced. "I was disappointed by Wilford's early sketch design. I had seen the Stuttgart gallery and I knew they could achieve the wow factor. But I was much happier with the final design. It achieves the access and openness we wanted. The auditoriums in particular are fantastic." Felicity Goodey commented: "We thought that as signature architects they'd throw tantrums, they'd make our lives a misery. But Michael and his team were wonderful. They'd always find a design solution to meet the budget."

Collaborative development

Not only did Michael Wilford and his designers have to respond to the views of Trust members and Stephen Hetherington's project team, but they also needed to take into account the different operational outcomes that arose from discussions between the Trust and the professional consultants advising on the architectural development of the building. Once the Lottery money was secured, Theatre Projects wrote the technical brief for performing arts in the building to meet the business and operational plan; Lord Cultural Resources did the same for the visual arts. Each spatial and functional element of The Lowry was described in detail and developed in close collaboration with the architect.

On the design of the Lyric Theatre auditorium, for example, Michael Wilford, Theatre Projects and the Trust worked closely together on the shape of the room to make it as intimate as possible. According to Jeremy Godden of Theatre Projects: "It's almost Georgian in concept. The walls are literally papered with people in tiers wrapping round to the stage." The auditorium was tiered, however, without sacrificing comfort. "Every presentation we made to The Lowry Centre Trust, they talked endlessly about comfort and sightlines," said Godden. "We set out a number of criteria for what we wanted to achieve and we developed computer-aided design models to show what the sightlines would be like - how much of the stage you could see from each seat. It was a crucial issue because The Lowry as a touring house will host different companies and shows with a whole range of sets."

While Theatre Projects liaised with the Trust on foyers, dressing rooms and the box office (which was relocated by the Trust following discussion), Lord Cultural Resources concentrated on the gallery spaces. "Salford's L S Lowry collection is intimate in scale, so we weren't looking for big spaces to hang giant contemporary works," explained Barry Lord. "The average size of a Lowry work is around 2 feet by 3 feet with many smaller, so the first principle was that these paintings and drawings should look good in the new galleries and allow visitors to focus on them. But we also needed enough space to show the entire collection at any one time, or show some Lowry work in the first gallery complemented by a mid-sized exhibition in the other galleries."

The configuration of the galleries was destined to undergo several revisions based on lengthy discussions between the main Lowry protagonists and international gallery directors. Controversially, Wilford and his team wanted the fourth in the sequence of L S Lowry galleries on the eastern flank of the building to be triangular in shape. Barry and Gail Lord were able to lend their support to this unconventional approach in discussions with the Trust, by citing precedents in Winnipeg Art Gallery, Canada, and in a Frankfurt gallery designed by Hans Hollein. The triangular gallery became a distinctive part of the scheme.

Acoustic arguments

A third consultant began to have an impact on the architectural form of the project by looking at it from the point of view of sound quality. Sandy Brown Associates, an experienced firm of acoustic consultants, was only brought onto The Lowry team in October 1996, several months after the Lottery award. "Ideally we like to get involved at the very beginning, at the feasibility stage," explained Kyri Kyriakides, a partner in Sandy Brown Associates who led the work on The Lowry Centre. "In this case, we were the last consultants on board. But as soon as we saw the Wilford building, we recognised it had the basis to be an extremely good theatre venue. Wilford had used the Edinburgh Festival Theatre as a reference point for his Lyric Theatre, and since we had worked on the acoustics of this venue, we knew it was a good place to start."

Kyriakides summarised the role of the acoustic consultant in any building as "controlling unwanted sounds and enhancing wanted sounds". At The Lowry, his analysis revealed that unwanted exterior noise could come from overhead aircraft or from the adjacent Metrolink and these needed to be sufficiently attenuated so that the visitor in the galleries or theatres would be unaware of them. Unwanted interior noise could result from inadequate sound insulation between bar and auditorium, for example, or from the rehearsal room above the Quays Theatre, or from building services such as air conditioning plant. But Kyriakides explained: "It is sometimes best not to reduce building service noise below a certain level as it can be useful in masking other noise at a low level."

To enhance wanted sounds, Sandy Brown Associates worked closely with the architect and the Lowry Centre Trust on the structural form and materials of the two auditoriums. (Lord specified the sound properties and reverberation times in the galleries.) In planning the acoustics of the Lyric Theatre, Kyriakides and his colleagues complemented study of the similar layout and capacity of the Edinburgh Festival Theatre with visits to other comparable theatres such as Glyndebourne (1,250 seats), Glasgow's Theatre Royal (1,566 seats) and the Grand Theatre, Leeds (1,603 seats).

Above: Kyri Kyriakides (right) and Ian Knowles from acousticians Sandy Brown Associates use polystyrene beads and a scale model to measure the volume of the Lyric Theatre at The Lowry.

Opposite: Illustration of the Lyric auditorium showing the perforated acoustic ceiling, the subject of intense debate.

Stephen Hetherington's business plan had specified that the acoustics of the auditorium should respond to a wide range of uses from opera to drama, but excluding orchestral concerts. So the acoustics needed to be variable and plans were developed to use retractable drapes to vary reverberation times (the amount of time taken for sound to die away). But Kyriakides was worried about a central aspect of Wilford's design for the Lyric auditorium - the ceiling line. "There are two things fundamental to the acoustics of any space - the volume of the space and the sound-absorbing properties of the space. The position of the ceiling usually defines the acoustic volumes of the space. If the volume is too small for its intended purpose, then it's impossible to do anything about the sound afterwards. Michael Wilford wanted the ceiling line to be at a particular point in the room for architectural reasons but we were very concerned that we couldn't design the acoustics needed in that space. There was a vigorous argument and it went on for some time."

Eventually a compromise was reached through a design innovation which was acceptable to everyone. "The solution was a suspended perforated metal ceiling, full of holes like a sieve.

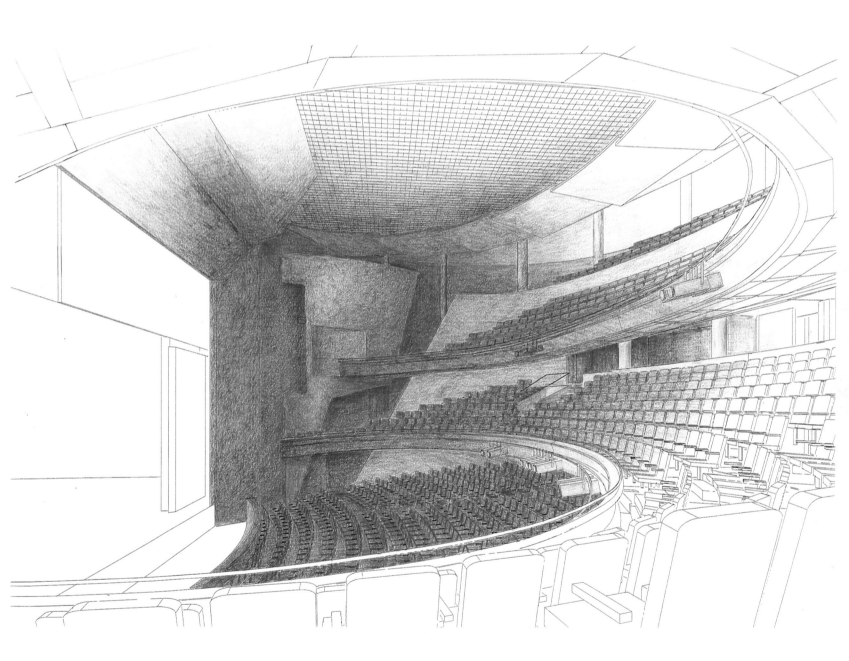

Elevations of the The Lowry
emphasising the strong,
almost nautical profile.

Top: **North elevation.**

Opposite top: **Cross section
through the Lyric Theatre.**

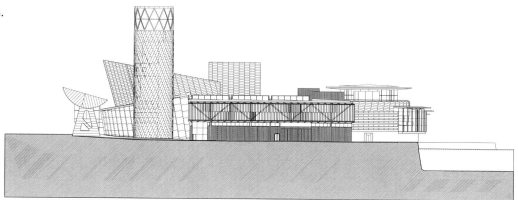

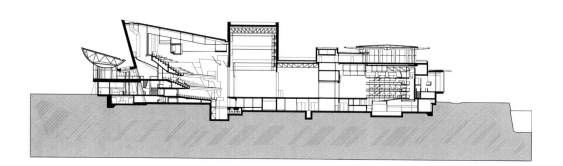

Bottom: **Long section
through auditoriums.**

Opposite bottom:
Plaza elevation.

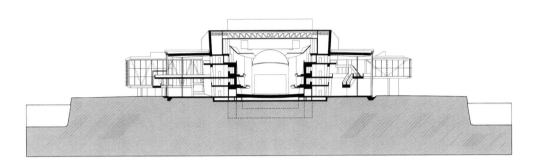

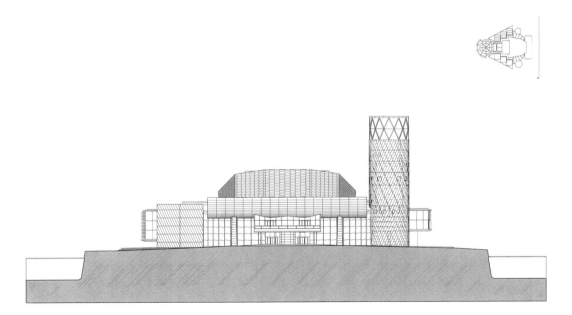

It is acoustically transparent in that sound doesn't see it, but the audience does," said Kyriakides. The real acoustic ceiling is behind that. Wilford's ceiling line, so essential to his architectural composition of the room, was preserved while Sandy Brown Associates was given the acoustic volumes it needed to make the acoustics variable in the auditorium and so meet the fundamentally different requirements of speech and music. (Shorter reverberation times can increase intelligibility of speech whereas longer reverberation times can improve the resonance of certain musical performances.) Central openings in the wire mesh for concealed stage lighting also enabled sound to travel through.

Where did the perforated ceiling solution come from? Wilford had seen a similar solution in the USA while Kyriakides explained: "We'd used the idea at St David's Hall, Cardiff." Interestingly, this venue is ranked by the eminent American acoustician Leo Beranek as one of the top eight concert halls in the world in terms of acoustics, which bodes well for sound quality at The Lowry. Also, St David's Hall was the only one of Beranek's top eight to be built in the 20th century.

Critical reception

Some of the heated debate over the architectural design proved to be a forerunner to later arguments over budgets between Trust, architect, contractors and consultants as the project reached the stage of fitting out the interior spaces. But the architect was usually able to hold the ring and reconcile the differences. As Gail Lord explained: "The genius of Michael Wilford & Partners was that the practice preserved the basic integrity and brilliance of the original sketch design while all the new facilities and modifications were being added."

Architectural critics tended to agree. Reviewing the scheme for *L'Arca* magazine, Maurizio Vogliazzo wrote: "The Lowry Centre is a perfectly packed parcel in which no space has been wasted." According to Vogliazzo, "The Lowry ... is not just startlingly beautiful with all its naval connotations; it is also highly functional thanks to the way its different parts are knit together, at times with what might even be described as majestic force ...." He concluded: "In actual fact the entire complex might be described as a lengthy, uninterrupted and highly varied architectural promenade, bearing in mind the physical layout of the building features and the way they are connected together."

The highly functional design of the building was not due simply to Wilford's own modernist inclinations but also to the fierce logic of The Lowry Centre Trust in driving the project forward by questioning every decision. As Wilford himself has written: "Architecture, as a pragmatic art, cannot be about style. The battle of style arises substantially from a deep suspicion of change." Perhaps the most impressive aspect of the architectural design is that the multi-functional requirements of the building are wrapped in a sculptural collage that retains its artistic flair despite all the changing demands placed upon it. Richard Carr observed in *Building Design*: "The complex looks like an architectural collage, jumbled and fragmented, but exciting and challenging."

One can make direct comparisons with other Stirling Wilford buildings, with other arts projects which are anchors for urban regeneration, or simply with other examples of innovative modern architecture. There is, for example, a familiar play on geometric shapes in Wilford's design for the new British Embassy in Berlin; a pronounced prow to the shiplike triangular form of the practice's scheme for Number One Poultry in the City of London; an emphasis on the relationship between plaza, promenade and parkland in Stirling Wilford's Temasek Polytechnic in Singapore, completed in 1995. Ideas that surface in other projects are honed by the Wilford practice at The Lowry.

Beyond the Stirling Wilford portfolio, one can see architectural solutions for new arts complexes in rundown urban districts in other parts of the world which are not dissimilar in form or spirit or

Lyric Theatre part of the model being built at Kandor Modelmakers, London, and delivered to The Lowry offices at West Pavilion, Salford Quays, July 1998.

outlook to The Lowry at Salford Quays. The public promenade is prominent and rhythmical in architect Christian de Portzamparc's east wing of the Cité de La Musique on the famous La Villette site in industrial Paris. Kiyonori Kikutake's Tokyo Edo Museum, meanwhile, hovers on four giant stilts over a regenerated district of the city as part of a design which involved reinserting historic canals to connect to Tokyo's Sukida River. Antoine Predock's Civic Arts Plaza at Thousand Oaks in California, with its tower, massing and cascade of terraces, gives civic focus to a drab stretch of brushland next to a busy freeway north of Los Angeles. Architectural strategies for regeneration are often shared internationally but made special by their local context.

Then there are the signature modern buildings to which Wilford's Lowry project relates: Frank Gehry's reflective Guggenheim Museum on the water in Bilbao; Kisho Kurakawa's Ehime Museum of Science in Japan, a seemingly random collage of geometric shapes at the foot of the mountains on Shikoku Island; Sir Richard Rogers's European Court of Human Rights, expressing the idea of transparency and openness in its form. But such comparisons only take you so far. In the end, The Lowry's architectural design is very much of itself; the building stands very much on its own terms against the tough, history-scarred landscape from which it clearly draws such inspiration.

The masterplan unravels

But if Michael Wilford was able to preserve the creative integrity of his building, the rational vision of the original masterplan slowly slipped from his grasp. Right from the start, The Lowry's triangular form had been generated by the adjacent geometries of the approaches to the building, the most important of which was the road which created a grand axis to the public plaza directly in front of the building. Wilford was anxious to preserve this avenue which made his building the hero, the stem rising to the arrow's head. Concepts for the commercial development essential to the future funding of The Lowry complex and the Virtual Reality Centre specified in the Lottery bid were both included in his plan, as part of his overall composition. But, despite being an adviser to the Trust on the masterplan for the site, Wilford's hopes of protecting the scheme within the logic of the three approaches were dashed.

The original projections for the scale of the commercial development contained in the feasibility brief to the architects came to be regarded as inadequate in terms of the revenue they would produce. Commercial developers wanted a larger retail-leisure scheme with a rectangular footprint on the site and there were demands to amend the masterplan. Eventually a commercial developer called Orbit, working with US architects RTKL and Bovis as management contractor, proposed a 500,000 square feet scheme which included a substantially enlarged retail-leisure complex for the site - the Lowry Galleria. This proposal rang alarm bells with the architects as the scale of this new scheme might dwarf The Lowry itself.

The Lowry Centre Trust faced one of its most difficult ethical decisions. Should it sacrifice Wilford's masterplan, in particular the approach to his building, to accommodate a commercial development which stood a better chance of financially underpinning the arts activities in The Lowry Centre? Or should it stand by the architect and his axis? It was a classic case of art versus mammon, aesthetics against economics. It was an issue that the Trust, wrapped up in the excitement of a scheme which Michael Wilford had done so much to visualise, would have preferred to avoid. In the event, it took the pragmatic decision to carve up the architectural plan in order to keep its business plan intact in terms of providing ongoing funds for the project from the retail-leisure development. At Salford City Council, Tony Struthers made the brutal assessment: "It's wonderful to be an aesthete but in the end you have to live with commercial reality."

The Orbit commercial development was incorporated into a new scheme by RTKL. Wilford's main axis to the building was abandoned and his masterplan left in tatters, leading the architect to comment with dignified understatement, "It's been a running battle but now the plan has lost its coherence." One questions whether the same call would have been made had the issue arisen in, say, Strasbourg or Stuttgart, while recognising the hard-hearted pragmatism that underscored the decision. In *The Independent*, architectural critic Nonie Niesewand described The Lowry within its new plan as "part of a gigantic business complex". She argued that the competing attractions of "cinemas, shops, offices and car parks leave The Lowry like a great stranded ship on a pier; at the widest stretch of the canal where, in the Thirties, ocean-going liners turned around." Other consultants working on The Lowry project also voiced their concerns. "It's a landmark building but are we actually going to be able to see it?" asked Jeremy Godden of Theatre Projects. "There will be a lot going on around it."

Digital World Centre

As if to add to Michael Wilford's chagrin, Orbit's architect RTKL also took over the architectural design of the Virtual Reality Centre, which was initially included as part of the overall commercial development package and then moved to a different part of the site to become a stand-alone scheme with a new name and purpose. According to Trust chairman Felicity Goodey, "It was Stephen Hetherington who alerted us to the flawed thinking at the heart of the Virtual Reality Centre, which was in our Lottery bid and to which we were committed. Stephen is an expert on IT but his argument was not technical - it was financial and related to the market. He said virtual reality was a cul-de-sac. He introduced the idea of a centre for a wider range of digital technologies."

To sort out the confusion surrounding the Virtual Reality Centre, Hetherington brought onto the project an American multimedia expert called Duffie White who had experience of planning visitor attractions and had lived in the Manchester area for several years. Between them, White

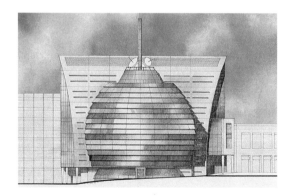

and Hetherington were eventually able to turn the project around. In this they were strongly supported by The Lowry property and construction director Steve Thorncroft who had joined the project from the Trafford Park Development Corporation as deputy chief executive, effectively Hetherington's right-hand man and vastly experienced in building. Again, it became a case of putting together a well-defined business plan to determine a more appropriate architectural brief. In the course of this process, the concept became the Digital World Centre with a broader remit.

A concept that began life as an educational goldfish bowl for Salford University VR researchers was turned by White into a spectacular multi-use showcase for the digital technologies, designed to engage local industry and education as well as be part of the global digital community. White saw the Digital World

Opposite: Original concept for the Digital World Centre by architects RTKL.

Above: Revised design following a move for the project to the south of the plaza.

Centre as complementing the Lowry's educational work and its links with the local community through a mixed programme of public displays and exhibitions, technical training courses, information seminars, international symposiums and professional conferences. He proposed a Digital World Society within the Centre, along the lines of the National Geographic Society, which would bring together business, government and academia in a powerful forum to discuss how digital developments could affect our world.

The partnership with Salford University remained integral to this vision. "We see all sorts of possibilities," said Professor Peter Brandon, who was not disheartened by the shift in emphasis.

"We anticipate that the Digital World Centre will be a shop window for our technologies and provide a public exhibition space for our work. It will enable us to rub shoulders with the major players and it will help in the natural transition from research into practice."

A separate project

The Digital World Centre was reformulated in its new guise as a £12 million project which will form an entirely separate architectural element within the overall scheme of The Lowry. IT services company EDS became The Lowry project's first founder partner with major sponsorship pledging £2 million of support over five years for The Lowry and the Digital World Centre. The European Regional Fund approved £1.87 million to nurture start-up businesses within the digital building. A competitive tender process undertaken by the Trust led to the appointment of RTKL, which successfully developed a scheme to meet the Trust's design criteria.

Like The Lowry itself, this also featured a triangular plan. But it was much smaller and very different in style and character to the main building, with a dramatic glass sail on the side of the structure. It was planned to sit to the left of the plaza tucked into the surviving axis to the new pedestrian bridge to Trafford Park, no longer a backdrop to Wilford's masterwork, more a sideshow. A total of 26,000 square feet of space was arranged over four floors: there was to be a public "digital discovery" exhibition space on the ground floor to view dynamic computer-generated environments; a theatre, auditorium and meeting facilities on the first floor; digital workshops and workspace on the second floor; a digital resource centre on the third floor; and offices and boardrom for the Digital World Society on the fourth floor.

White reflected on the difficulties of arriving at a suitable design: "Is it an exhibition centre? A thinktank? An educational site? It is all of those and more." The succession of delays and rethinks over the purpose, form and funding of the Digital World Centre meant that it became a stand-alone facility with its own timetable for completion past the opening of The Lowry. With more work on the commercial requirements of the building, it became clear that its footprint needed to be larger - more like the 50,000 square feet that could be achieved across on the other side of the plaza.

This further element was pitched into the already strained and difficult negotations between Salford City Council, The Lowry and the commercial developers Orbit. But agreement was worked through and the site to the south of the plaza secured. Further to this, Stephen Hetherington and Steve Thorncroft achieved the commercial viability of the new proposition and Duffie White continued to pioneer the idea of the Digital World Society. Thorncroft began testing process to make sure everything was in place for a start on-site. The Digital World Centre remains integral to the whole enterprise - a truly millennial aspect of the total project as a place to showcase digital technologies alongside the performing and visual arts.

Bridge to the future

Although Michael Wilford's original masterplan, which included his first concepts for the Digital World Centre, was subject to radical revision, the architect tried to exert his influence to greater effect over the design of The Lowry footbridge linking Salford Quays to Trafford Park and the designated site for the Imperial War Museum North, designed by Daniel Libeskind. The contract to design and construct the footbridge was won by a local Salford engineering firm, Parkman, following an international competition which attracted 70 applicants. Parkman had worked extensively on such projects as motorway bridges and had forged close links with

Top: Duffie White, a multimedia expert brought in to give substance to the idea behind the Digital World Centre.

Above: Alan Stevens, chief executive of IT services company EDS, studies plans for the Digital World Centre on the day his company pledges support for The Lowry project.

a Spanish design company, Casado of Madrid. Their joint competition entry proposed a lifting bridge with four curved towers in the shape of large questions marks.

According to Parkman's Bill Middleton, "The people from Casado came over to have a look at the site and take photographs. They then went back to Spain to come up with some conceptual designs. When they returned with a completed design, we thought 'Good grief!' It was totally different from anything we'd ever seen before. After that first reaction of amazement, we were convinced we'd be in with a chance. Nothing was changed, we just worked out the engineering implications of actually operating it. That was then submitted as our competition entry."

The striking Parkman-Casado proposal won the competition, but in his role as architectural consultant to the Lowry Centre Trust, Michael Wilford raised objections to the design of the towers: "The towers were too huge and solid. I persuaded the Trust to ask for design modifications." So Parkman and Casado duly went back to the computer screen to create more restrained and less bulky tower profiles. "We were understandably disapppointed that the design wasn't accepted in its entirety but you have to be flexible about these things," said Bill Middleton, whose firm increasingly saw the potential of relating to the educational remit of The Lowry by constructing a lifting bridge that would be explicit in explaining its own function.

One might see in Michael Wilford's intervention over the footbridge the despairing act of an architect trying to maintain standards and exercise design control over a large and complex project beginning to slip from his grasp. But nobody could doubt what The Lowry project had come to mean to him, nor fail to understand why he would fight so hard to achieve his architectural goals. "The Lowry is very important to me and to the practice," he explained. "It will be the first major project we've done without James Stirling. Having worked with Jim and been his partner for so long, I now have the opportunity to forge a new direction." The Lowry also represented a new beginning in architectural terms, as well as personal ones. "In Britain, there's an atmosphere where it is almost imposible to do anything that is wholly contemporary," said Wilford. "But I think the design of The Lowry is really quite radical and I'm amazed we've got the project as far as we have. This building makes no concessions. There's nothing to limit you and that's what is so wonderful about the site."

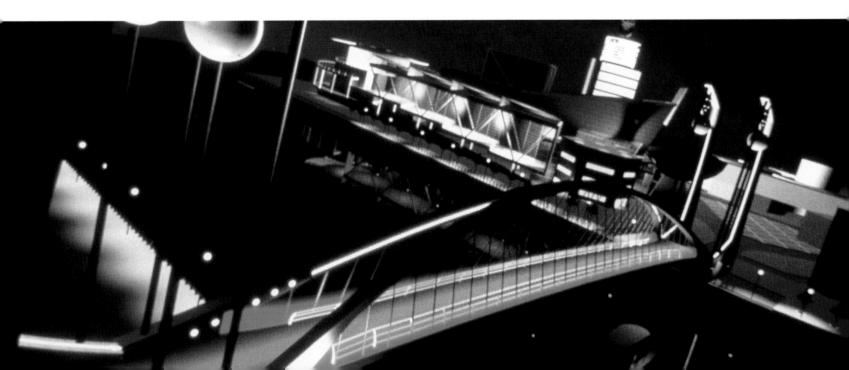

4 INTO CONSTRUCTION

"Great and unique architecture comes
with a price. The engineering and construction
challenges are all the harder."

Steve Thorncroft, Property and Construction Director, The Lowry Centre Trust

Arts facilities are notoriously difficult to build. They are invariably large structures but, unlike offices or department stores, the floors don't repeat; levels don't appear to relate; services are problematic; and large interior volumes need to be supported without columns or beams that might obscure sightlines. As The Lowry went on site, arts building veterans involved in the project were queuing up to tell anyone who would listen how contractors are naive about the difficulties of building theatres, how they start out thinking it will be fun and end up driven to distraction, how there's never enough money to complete, and how the building will never open on time. So it is to the credit of everyone responsible for building The Lowry - design team, engineers, contractors, project managers and construction workers - that they remained undaunted by the difficulties of the scheme and wrestled continuously with the eternal triangle of budget, deadline and quality to achieve the results that Michael Wilford's exceptional architectural design demanded. According to David Porter of management services company Gleeds, which played a key role as project managers, "When it's a fantastic building like this, everyone raises their game."

Construction of The Lowry would prove to be every bit as complex and difficult as putting together the funding package had been. The problems of raising the money as a patchwork from so many different sources would be mirrored at a later stage by the problems of coordinating and sequencing so many different aspects of the project. According to Steve Thorncroft, the construction management expert brought in to run the building work for The Lowry Centre Trust project team, the uniqueness of Michael Wilford's design also contributed to making the going tougher. "Great and unique architecture comes with a price," said Thorncroft, who assumed his role as property and construction director at The Lowry on 1 January 1998. "The engineering and construction challenges are all the harder."

Bidding for the contract

At least Bovis Construction, the company which built The Lowry, went in with its eyes open. It was fresh from building the Manchester Arena, as well as the new Glyndebourne Opera House, and in Bovis North (later Bovis Lend Lease) director Dennis Bate it had a leader whose commitment to the project went way beyond contractual obligation. "We saw The Lowry as a landmark project for the whole region," explained Bate, who was born and bred in the Manchester area and played a key role in developing the city's infrastructure for the 2000 Olympic bid. Bate saw himself as a mover and shaker in the region. "I always saw the potential of Manchester," he insisted - and he was successful in establishing Bovis, a southern building firm by tradition, as a major player in the North-West.

The Lowry would test his local convictions to the limit. Bate first learned about the project when he attended a Hallé concert sponsored by BT in 1994, at which Felicity Goodey stood up and spoke about what was planned on Pier 8 at Salford Quays. "Immediately I could see the vision and I bought into it," said Bate. "I believed they would deliver and I wanted to build it." The problem, as Bate saw it, was that several builders would chase the project. There would be a fierce bout of fee-cutting to win it and then a slow adversarial slog during the project to claw back costs from the various construction packages that would be coordinated. This did not appeal. So Bate decided to look at things from a different angle. "I needed to get a special edge to win the project and demonstrate my commitment. So I chose to get involved with The Lowry's adjacent commercial development as a developer. That would really differentiate Bovis from our competitors. If we could secure the development, then we'd be well placed to secure The Lowry as builders of the whole site."

Working with sister company P&O Development through Bovis Urban Regeneration, Bate pitched for the commercial development with a scheme that he felt would be sympathetic to The Lowry flagship. "We tried to be as flexible and imaginative as possible," he said. The bid was successful, but that didn't mean The Lowry construction contract automatically fell into his lap. What it did mean, however, was that Bate found himself at the top table where he was able to demonstrate his grasp of the project. For example, he met the Millennium Commission to convince them that the commercial development plan was robust enough to provide £350,000 each year to subsidise The Lowry. "Bovis became part of the jigsaw that slotted together to secure the Lottery money for The Lowry," said Bate.

When The Lowry construction project was formally advertised in June 1996, the Bovis team studied Michael Wilford's drawings carefully to work out how best to put the building together, visited the Staatsgalerie in Stuttgart to observe the quality that Wilford demanded, and submitted financial, logistical, technical and programme proposals to The Lowry Centre Trust, as well as details of its track record and the team that would build The Lowry. The important role of project director was given to Peter Roberts, an experienced construction professional 21 years with Bovis, who had worked on the Manchester Arena. Bovis won the job. "We signed the contract on Christmas Eve 1996," said Roberts. "It really went to the wire."

Non-adversarial construction

Signing a construction contract is usually like going to war. Even the ebullient Dennis Bate admitted, "Construction is a battlefield." But Bovis is a believer in non-adversarial contracting. Since 1968, when it built the landmark John Player factory in Nottingham, the company has pioneered management contracting. This is a sophisticated process of works contracting: the construction company is paid a fee - a percentage of overall building costs - to manage the contract and

Above: Bovis project director Peter Roberts in a project meeting with Lowry Centre Trust chairman Felicity Goodey.

Right: Michael Wilford explains the layout of the building to journalists during a site visit by the media in October 1998.

coordinate all works on site. The project is divided into a series of work packages involving different trades. Bovis works with the design team to implement these packages and goes to the market for bids to complete each package. Management contracting as a process enabled work to start on site without full working drawings, which was an advantage given the deadlines that had to be hit, but there were also downsides in terms of cost that would be discovered later.

The Lowry's total construction budget was around £60 million. This was largely public money and could not be exceeded. David Porter of Gleeds explained, "A fixed budget means you can't overshoot because there's no more money. You can't undershoot either or you have to give money back. You need to hit it right on the bullseye." To achieve this, Gleeds liaised constantly with all members of the building team and especially with its client, Steve Thorncroft. To keep the programme to schedule, it looked to Bovis and its sub-contractors; to adhere to the costs schedule, it worked with quantity surveyors Davis Langdon & Everest; on issues of quality, it liaised with Michael Wilford & Partners. "We sit right in the middle of that time-cost-quality triangle," explained Porter. "Gleeds is the glue that holds it all together. Only Michael Wilford and Theatre Projects were appointed to The Lowry before us. When Peter Roberts shouts, 'Where are the drawings?' or when Michael Wilford says he can't get samples from a sub-contractor - we're in there to sort it out. It's all about relationships."

Managing the funders

Steve Thorncroft meanwhile was faced with the difficult task of liaising with all the different funders as the budget was expended. "They all have different requirements and legal conditions to satisfy. It's right that we should be accountable but there's no escaping that it's awfully difficult to manage," he explained, as the monthly monitoring began to take its toll. Stephen Hetherington was only too glad to hand over this heavy responsibility to Thorncroft and other members of the team. At the Arts Council, Lottery Panel chairman Prue Skene admitted: "We're all on a steep learning curve with The Lowry. Putting three different mechanisms into place to monitor the project on behalf of three different funders is difficult, but none of us would be in this business if it was just plain sailing."

Thorncroft had worked for 11 years on the other side of the Manchester Ship Canal with Trafford Park Development Corporation, where he had been responsible for delivering £170 million of projects associated with the regeneration of Trafford Park, including reclamation and landscaping, new roads and buildings. But The Lowry was the single largest project he had ever managed. "When I started, there was an army of well-qualified consultants on board but nobody to manage them, nobody to speak their language," said Thorncroft. "Standing back and looking at it, my biggest fear was that it was an extremely tight programme. If we lost time, the budget or the quality could suffer. The balance between programme, money and quality is always tough to resolve."

Spanners in the works

But what could go wrong with The Lowry construction project to make the programme slip or send costs skywards? Bovis knew soon enough. Early researches of the site revealed that the land was heavily contaminated. The project dawdled in a low gear while Bovis sorted that out. Peter Roberts was also concerned by other challenges posed by the triangular site: "Having water on two sides impeded access, although there were less traffic constraints. We were building close to local residences. The water was newly cleaned which meant we needed to be extra careful in how we discharged waste. And the water table was high, which meant the basement was below the water table and this affected the sequence required to waterproof the building."

Above: Lowry property and construction director Steve Thorncroft (second right) puts his point across during a site visit.

Opposite: The site photographed in November 1997, a mass of steel reinforcing rods ready for yet more concrete.

There was a further complication. The dock walls, affected by cranes vibrating over many years, were not stable. So the decision was made to leave them load-free. Instead, 803 concrete piles were sunk right down to the rock bed to make the building stable in its own right, irrespective of movement in the dock walls. These vertical piles, 26 metres deep at the lowest point, were made by sinking a rig drill auger into the ground using a hollow drill. Concrete was then pumped through this machine and the drill gradually pulled out, leaving concrete to fill up the hole left behind. Achieving the required accuracy was difficult. Uncharted underground obstructions included timber wharfing, warehouse foundations and even débris dating from before the excavation of the Manchester Ship Canal in 1894.

"We looked hard at the building to see where it could catch us out," said Roberts. "We decided that the key design problem was in the interfaces. That's where things could go wrong if we overlooked certain details. If the steelwork was not level, for instance, it was not waterproof and that might lose us weeks." Dennis Bate too recognised that Wilford's building geometries were exacting, especially the relationship between the complex concrete walls, structural steel girders and glass façades. "Design needs to give some tolerance," said Bate. "There's no point in a design you can't achieve. So we had to work very closely with the architect and the different trade contractors to achieve the right adjacencies."

David Porter at Gleeds described the interfaces as "amazingly complicated - probably the most complex we've been involved with." But there was no question that the design ambition should be curtailed just to make it more easily buildable. Indeed Peter Roberts was acutely aware of the artistic image of the building: "Making the connections delicate so that the architect only gets a hint of steel was a tough challenge, given the structures we were dealing with."

Engineering challenges

Among the biggest headaches was the construction of the dramatic sloping concrete wall to the Lyric Theatre, which cost £500,000 alone to build. "It's tricky, it's leaning, it's complex," said Roberts. "It's not even solid, because there are large perforations through the structure to create openings for landings and staircases to poke out." Consulting engineers Buro Happold, widely recognised as one of Europe's most technically competent and imaginative consultancies in this field, had been appointed in November 1995 to work closely with Michael Wilford to realise his designs. According to David Hull, the Buro Happold partner in charge of The Lowry project, "In terms of structural engineering, the two theatres presented the greatest challenges."

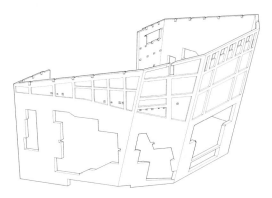

The Lyric Theatre is surrounded by a 28-metre high reinforced concrete wall which wraps around on seven sides. The two flank walls and the return walls at the stage are vertical, but the front walls to the foyer slope at an angle of 17 degrees. With openings in this structure to allow stairs to punch through and cantilever balconies to extend back over the main foyer, the engineers puzzled over how to make it all work. The solution entailed making the 600mm-thick lower sections of the wall very highly stressed and reducing the upper sections of the wall to 200mm thickness with stiffeners; these act in a horizontal band to tie the raking sections back to the vertical flank walls. The thinner panels allow services to run within an overall 600mm thickness to gain access to the foyer roof.

The design of the Quays Theatre, with its demands for three different staging configurations and four levels of seating within a horseshoe shape, also tested Buro Happold's ingenuity. The seating hangs from a substantial roof structure which also supports a rehearsal room. Buro Happold proposed that 20 Macalloy bars, each 13 metres long and 40mm in diameter, should form the suspension structure for the exposed steelwork frame of the seating. The architect wanted the steelwork left exposed as part of the design. But these proposals sat uneasily with strict fire regulations for a 450-seat public theatre, which would have required thick protective paint or a cladding surround under normal one-hour fire resistance rules.

However Buro Happold's engineers were able to convince Salford City Council that the unprotected steelwork frame would provide sufficient fire resistance and would not collapse. Buro Happold fielded its own fire engineering specialist, Fedra, which used computer modelling to work out every conceivable fire hazard - including a fire in an adjacent support hangar which subjected the unprotected steelwork to its worst-case scenario. "We were not governed by prescriptive regulations because this type of building had not been done before," explained

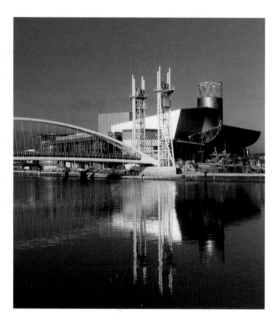

David Hull. "The normal rules didn't apply and, to some extent, we had to make them up." The decision to accept Buro Happold's case not only made the architect happy but it also shaved £100,000 off the budget - which is what the additional fire protection would have cost. Buro Happold also considered sustainability issues, incorporating innovative solutions to reduce energy consumption and moderate the internal environment. Its use of specialist daylight modelling techniques also helped to create appropriate conditions in The Lowry galleries.

Cladding the building

Michael Wilford's design development to clad the upper part of his building with reflective stainless steel tiles, instead of the purple cladding in the original design, made additional demands on the construction process. These shingles had never been used before in Britain, although, following the success of Frank Gehry's Guggenheim Museum in Bilbao using German tiles manufactured by Temasex, they are now much more widely recognised and talked about. To remain within budget, a proprietary cladding system could not be specified. Instead, each tile needed to be cut locally, so cladding contractor Broderick took on a small industrial unit for this purpose. Each home-made tile is nearly 2 metres long, 1 metre wide and 0.4mm thick. Its design was evolved from a series of folding cardboard models developed by the architect.

Cladding the building with individual stainless steel shingles was not the nightmare it might have been, and as the structure took shape, locals remarked on the way The Lowry was beginning to reflect land and sky. This was a key motivating factor for Michael Wilford, as well as for fellow architect Peter Hunter, who had been among the first to see the potential of the site. But after the initial blow of the contaminated ground, other setbacks hit the Bovis team - higher than expected tenders, bad winter weather, mistakes by installers, even a nest of mistle thrushes whose merciless attacks on passing workers halted the project and briefly became headline news.

Peter Roberts was proud of the ability of his young, enthusiastic Bovis team - average age 35 - to emerge from the low points of the project to keep going. Things never eased up. From the moment prior to starting on site, when the quantity surveyors handed Gleeds a cost plan that was £6 million over budget, the race was on to take cost out of the project while ensuring that the building would open on time and be of the required quality. The way to achieve this, explained Porter, was through a "continual process of value engineering" - design changes, tenders and

Aerial view of The Lowry
in March 2000.
The foundations of the new
Imperial War Museum -
North can be seen underway
on the opposite bank.

construction packages were all worked on together to find the right solutions, a necessity of the management contracting process. "In other words, we are constructing a building that is still being designed," said Porter. Nobody doubted how stressful this could be. As one of the Bovis team told a visiting journalist: "Nothing here is straightforward. I can't wait to go off and build a shed."

Lowry footbridge

The Lowry Centre was not, however, the only construction project on the Pier 8 site. Work on the new Lowry footbridge, to link The Lowry to Trafford Park Wharfside and the site of the new Imperial War Museum - North, was also going on. This too experienced ups and downs over cost and quality, although, as Steve Thorncroft pointed out, time constraint was less of a factor. At the outset, when contractors were asked to submit bids to build the competition-winning footbridge designed by Salford engineering firm Parkman, in association with Spanish design company Casado, the lowest of the bids came in some £2 million over the £5 million set budget. There seemed no way round this impasse. Contractor Christiani Nielsen had made the lowest bid, but, according to Christiani Nielsen project manager Simon Leffan, The Lowry footbridge was "dead in the water".

What resurrected the footbridge was a value-engineering exercise not unlike the process taking place in The Lowry building itself. In the face of Michael Wilford's criticisms, Parkman's redesign of the imposing towers shaped like question marks replaced curved pre-stressed concrete with less visually dominant lattice-framed tubular steel towers, which were much less expensive to produce. Workshops were held to find other ways to reduce costs, resulting in a change to the bridge's lifting mechanism. A single bespoke electric motor was replaced with six smaller standard hydraulic ones: this design change saved £100,000 as well as providing a system that would be more easily maintained and repaired. A further £100,000 was saved when the construction team decided not to demolish a hollow concrete structure sitting precisely where they wanted to land the bridge but to insert concrete piles through holes drilled in the structure.

The new-look 92-metre-wide footbridge bridge took shape, 250 tonnes in weight and with a vertical hydraulic lift capability to 23 metres above water level. Its four tubular lattice-framed towers, 32 metres in height, were designed with 60 tonne counterweights and winding gear left exposed and on show as an educational attraction for Lowry visitors. Steel foundation beams were inserted to distribute the weight of the bridge towers to those parts of the quay able to take the weight. Dynamic lighting was also integrated into the structure, to illuminate a symbol of innovative design and engineering despite the requirement to trim costs. According to Bill Middleton of Parkman, "It's an excellent project - a real one-off. The bridge stands almost as high as the Quay West office block. Even with its modified design, it's really quite striking - a new landmark for the area."

Construction of the footbridge, photographed in June 1998 from Quay West. The north side towers are in position, the south side towers are being put together piece by piece.

Erecting the footbridge

Once the design and construction details were settled, the task of erecting the new footbridge in place over the Manchester Ship Canal fell to Christiani Nielsen. The contractors were only allowed a four-day closure of the Canal - and faced financial penalties if they exceeded that time limit. This meant that the towers had to be erected first and then the bridge span lifted into place, rather than the entire structure built as a whole. Simon Leffan of Christiani Nielsen explained

Gerald Kaufman, MP (centre) with other members of the Culture, Media and Sport Select Committee on the site, July 1998.

that the simplest way to do this would have been to build the bridge span immediately adjacent to the quay on the Pier 8 side and then push it out between the towers. But temporary building contractors' offices blocked this route, so instead the bridge span was constructed next to a dry dock 300 metres further up the Canal, lifted onto a large steel pontoon and floated back down to the site of the four towers.

On the north side, there was space for cranes to lift up the two north towers in one go, but on the south side, this was not possible. So the two southside towers were broken down into three smaller sections to be brought by road, lifted and built into place. Taking the bridge span from the steel barge, lifting it into alignment with the towers and attaching it to the cables of the hydraulic system was the most critical part of the operation, a tricky manoeuvre which had Steve Thorncroft and the rest of The Lowry team on the edge of their seats. Once in place, there was a month of commissioning and testing the bridge - "making it go up and down like a yo-yo", as Simon Leffan put it. Despite the obstacles placed in its way, which even included a Second World War bomb alert (bomb casing fragments were found in the quayside), the project was successful. An important piece of The Lowry jigsaw was slotted firmly into place. "These pieces of civil engineering are never easy," observed Thorncroft. "The Lowry footbridge took longer than expected but it is a quality statement of architecture and engineering."

Measuring up to stiff criteria

With the footbridge to Trafford Park finally open and the main Lowry building rising fast against the skyline, the design and construction process was beginning to earn plaudits. Writing in *Building* magazine in November 1998, Gerald Kaufman, MP for Manchester Gorton and chairman of the Culture, Media and Sport Select Committee, observed: "There aren't too many buildings with this hypnotic power: the Taj Mahal undoubtedly; St Mark's in Venice, yes; here in Britain, Durham and Salisbury cathedrals. Will The Lowry Centre be another? I hope so, but we cannot be sure until the whole complex is completed. What is certain is that hardly any other recent building in Britain measures up to this, admittedly testing, criterion."

With so much progress to show, Stephen Hetherington invited arts journalists to view what was happening on site. After one such tour, *Sunday Telegraph* music critic Michael Kennedy likened The Lowry to "a surrealist power station, light and airy, a dazzle of glass and steel". This was an uncanny echo of the remark made by Salford chief executive Roger Rees to Jim Stirling right at the start that the scheme resembled Heysham Power Station. Clearly, Rees was a visionary back in 1992. Writing in spring 1999, exactly one year before opening, Kennedy told his readers: "If you still think of Salford as the dirty end of the Manchester Ship Canal, you are several years out of date." But as the building project raced towards its conclusion, there were mixed feelings in the Bovis camp. "The finish of every project excites me and depresses me at the same time because you lose your baby," said Dennis Bate. Bovis project director Peter Roberts was more pragmatic: "When the public comes into this building they won't have a clue what it's taken to build it, and neither will they care."

5 WORK IN PROGRESS

"Once complete The Lowry will be photographed time and again... but it's the process of construction that I find so fascinating. Every day the site changes and on each visit you make a unique, unrepeatable record. It's like capturing a piece of history."

Len Grant, photographer

SEPTEMBER | 1997

Right & opposite: Each of the 803 piling columns which sink right down to the rock bed to make the building stable is excavated and "capped".

JULY | 1997

Below right: The triangular "diaphragm wall" is excavated using giant grabs that plunge down and dig using their own weight.

JULY | 1997

Previous page: The steel frame for the Lyric Theatre foyer is lifted into place.

DECEMBER | *1997*

Opposite: With water on two sides, a concrete "diaphragm wall" is constructed parallel to the dockside.

Opposite: Views of early construction and of the triangular site, with the Quays Theatre at the apex and the Lyric in the foreground. The ground is prepared for the Artworks Gallery to be built on the left flank and the Lowry Galleries on the right.

**Opposite: Semi-circular
structure of the Quays
Theatre from which the
steel framework for the
seating will be "hung".**

**Right: The Lyric Theatre's
stage and fly tower take shape.**

**Previous pages:
The Quays Theatre,
which takes the brunt of
the wind as it comes
down the canal, and foyers
under construction.**

Opposite: View of the framework in place for the Lyric Theatre, with the stage at bottom right.

Right: Sequence showing the first lift of the steel roof for the Quays Theatre at The Lowry.

Previous pages: The steel frame for the Lyric Theatre.

The Lyric Theatre

Opposite: Steel roof girders are lifted into position.

Top right: The theatre's sloping rear wall.

Centre right: The concrete tiers in place on the circle level with the steel frame of the upper circle still exposed.

Bottom right: Installing steel beams in the theatre's foyer areas.

SEPTEMBER | *1998*

Erectors from steel specialist William Hare piece together the frame for the Compass Room above the Quays Theatre.

**Opposite: Constructing
The Lowry footbridge.
Each of the two south
towers was brought to
the quayside in sections,
to be built on site.**

**Previous pages:
The steel frame for
the "hexagon" adjacent
to the Artworks Gallery
is fixed in place.**

JANUARY | 1998

**For each of the four towers
of The Lowry footbridge,
63 tonnes of tubular steel
are fabricated at
Fairport Engineering in
Adlington, Lancashire.**

The bridge deck for The Lowry footbridge is built at Manchester Dry Docks, less than a kilometre along the Manchester Ship Canal from The Lowry. The deck is then manoeuvred onto a pontoon ready for its short trip up the canal, as construction workers anticipate a tricky operation.

The bridge deck for
The Lowry footbridge is
successfully towed to the
site and positioned between
the towers, after a previous
attempt the day before
had been aborted due
to strong winds.

The Lowry footbridge – "a quality statement of architecture and engineering". It rises in just three minutes to allow large vessels into Salford Quays. When down, it provides a pedestrian link between The Lowry and the Imperial War Museum-North on the opposite bank.

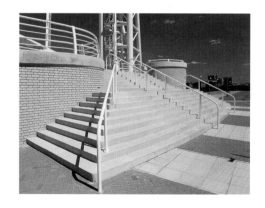

Above: Roofing work under way at The Lowry, including the installation of glass roof panels above the internal promenade.

Opposite: The exterior fly tower walls are prepared for stainless steel cladding.

Stainless steel panels are
installed on the fly tower.

JUNE | 1999

Opposite: View of new stainless steel cladding, which has invited inevitable comparisons with Frank Gehry's Guggenheim Museum in Bilbao. The original cladding was purple but was changed during design development.

NOVEMBER 1998 | JULY 1999

Previous pages: The Study Tower in construction. Steel erectors use a "man-rider" basket to complete the criss-cross framework.

View of the complete Lowry
development, including footbridge
and building, from the west across
the Manchester Ship Canal.

APRIL | 1999

Opposite: View of the first floor level of the building with the Lyric Theatre wall on the left and the steel framework linking the sloping exterior wall.

MAY | 1999

Above: Scaffolding fills the Lyric Theatre as work is completed on the problematic "acoustic ceiling".

Sanding the concrete base
for the promenade route
through the building.

The heavy kit is brought in to
prepare the foyer floors as
The Lowry gears up for its
spring 2000 opening.

JULY | *1999*

Above: Sealing the glass panels in the Artworks interactive gallery.

Opposite: Completing the Quays Theatre foyer, part of the "internal promenade".

The steel frame for The Lowry's
distinctive canopy stands exposed
to the Salford skyline.

**Above: A dredger cleans
the Manchester Ship Canal
against the backdrop of
The Lowry building
and footbridge.**

**Opposite:
The complex geometric
forms of The Lowry near
completion, set against
the tower blocks of the
Salford district of Pendleton.
Local people are looking
for the development to
bring economic benefits
to the area.**

Previous pages: The stainless
steel cladding is in place.

Opposite: The exposed skin of
the Study Tower, set to be a
distinctive feature on the
Salford Quays skyline.

1997 | 2000

Thirty views of the site as it developed over time. These photographs were taken from the Quay West office development on Trafford Wharfside.

6 PLANNING THE INTERIORS

"We're planning a department store for the arts which is non-élitist and not defined by social class. It's like Selfridges, where you can buy a pencil or a fur coat...."

Stephen Hetherington, The Lowry Chief Executive

With the design and construction of The Lowry well advanced, the focus of attention began to switch to what would be happening inside the building. Planning of the interior spaces which would house the daring mix of performing and visual arts in a sequence of theatres and galleries had been developing for some time under the direction of Stephen Hetherington and The Lowry Centre Trust. As the author of the business plan for The Lowry, Hetherington was in a unique position to influence the outcomes, putting into practice theories about the arts which, as he explained, "have been inside my head for years and which I've debated endlessly in boardrooms, pubs and cafés". His view of The Lowry was essentially defined by his belief that everyone can engage in artistic creativity, that listening to rap music on a Walkman is as valid as attending an opera, and that any arts venue must do more than just be a production facility.

Central to Hetherington's philosophy is a distinction between artistic production, for which he believes it is perfectly valid to provide subsidy, and presentation, for which he believes it is not. The Lowry, he argued, should largely be about presentation and should therefore be financially self-sufficient in programming. According to Hetherington, the post-war consensus about theatre and the visual arts in Britain has been tied too directly to the system of subsidy. "I see subsidy as a form of censorship in which a small group of people decide what is good or appropriate for the mass of the people," he explained. "The arts have been hijacked by the funding system, but they should be about creativity, not about subsidy. I want The Lowry to be a township which fairly fizzes with creativity. Its landscape should be multi-faceted in character, allowing people to come into the building to form their own views and experience their own sense of creativity."

This idea of the diverse township - a bustling arts marketplace of public promenades, rooms and plazas - reconciled any conflict in Hetherington's mind between the performing arts theatres, which are essentially receiving spaces for touring productions, and the gallery spaces, which work in relation to a visual art collection on site. In addition to this analogy, Hetherington also advanced another model for his vision. "We're planning a department store for the arts which is non-élitist and not defined by social class. It's like Selfridges, where you can buy a pencil or a fur coat...." he explained. "We have to buy well, display well and sell well. We need experts to stock the shelves but we don't need experts to grow or make the produce."

One can immediately see an inherent tension in Hetherington's approach. On the one hand, there is the desire to be financially strong and self-sufficient at The Lowry, which explains why early proposals for a resident theatre company (which would have required varying degrees of subsidy to maintain) were ruled out. On the other, creating your own sense of identity and independence as an arts showcase requires some measure of artistic origination, which strays into the area of artistic production. Hetherington was adamant that a balancing act could be maintained - that The Lowry could assert its self-worth artistically while standing on its own two feet financially. To do that, however, required a clever twist to running artistic policy.

A triumvirate in charge

Hetherington always anticipated that a triumvirate of managers would run artistic policy at The Lowry, and that he would be flanked by a theatres director responsible for all aspects of the performing arts and a galleries director doing likewise for the visual arts. These were the experts who would stock his shelves. By October 1998, these appointments were made and the effect on The Lowry project was to take the planning of the interiors and of the programme to a new level of intensity.

Robert Robson was recruited from the Scottish theatre scene to become theatres director; David Alston, a senior curator at the National Museums and Galleries of Wales, was appointed galleries director. Hetherington commented: "I see my job now as pouring on water and fertiliser so it all grows, while adhering to the business plan. When you engage clever people, they take ownership of different parts of the township, and the town changes." Robson and Alston quickly made their mark, bringing their own energy, ideas and perspectives to the work already achieved and the decisions still to be made.

For the consultant team working on The Lowry, these appointments were long overdue. "I understand the reasons why Stephen Hetherington could not have all his senior leadership

people on board from the beginning, but the arrival of David Alston was a huge relief for us," commented Gail Lord of visual art consultants Lord Cultural Resources. "Until his introduction to the project, there was no real end user for the gallery development. David is the one who will have to make these spaces work as the artistic director of the programme. In truth we could have done with him a year earlier."

There was a similar response from Theatre Projects, which claimed its work on the two theatre auditoriums lacked a focus until the arrival of Robert Robson. "The Lowry does not have a resident theatre company for which we could create special lighting and sound systems," explained Jeremy Godden of Theatre Projects. "It's a venue with a workhorse system designed to be efficient, uncomplicated and smooth so that big touring productions can come in and out on a weekly basis. Our problem was that we didn't have a technical theatre person to relate to. We were designing for a Trust, which was difficult. When Robert came, it was fantastic; the whole project came alive for us."

Hetherington disputes that a vacuum existed before the arrival of Alston and Robson, citing his own extensive technical theatre experience and the role of Salford Art Gallery's curators in advising Lord on the Lowry collection. But nevertheless it is clear how much the development of a new arts venue is a "people business" whose progress is dependent on forging very real human relationships. For Theatre Projects and Lord, both ploughing through endless technical detail in realising the interior facilities, fresh faces with independent views were welcome indeed.

The theatres remit

Robson's curriculum vitae made him a strong candidate for The Lowry theatres post, in that his experience in the theatre unusually combined community involvement and mixed-arts programming with commercial operation. After university and professional training, he had begun his career in the late 1970s as a community drama worker working on the Easterhouse Festival in Glasgow, encouraging local people to use their own talents and develop their own environment. In 1983 he was appointed artistic director of the Cumbernauld Theatre 15 miles from Glasgow, responsible for mixed programming across a range of artforms, including educational work in schools; and in 1990, he became festival director of Mayfest, Glasgow's international arts festival.

Top: The new Lowry management team go on site - Steven Hetherington (left), David Alston (centre) and Robert Robson.

Above: Lowry theatres director Robert Robson reflects on the decisions ahead.

Four years later Robson crossed the fence from subsidised into commercial theatre as theatre director of the 1,400-seat city-centre His Majesty's Theatre in Aberdeen. By the time the Lowry post was advertised in spring 1998, he was general manager of performing arts venues for Aberdeen City Council. "I knew about The Lowry from the very early days," says Robson, "and I always wanted to be part of something starting from scratch. That was the big attraction, being in at the beginnning. There are all sorts of possibilities, which makes it quite scary but really exciting."

Below: The interior of the Lyric Theatre during construction and nearing completion.

Part of the interview process involved a visit by Stephen Hetherington to Aberdeen to look over the three venues for which Robson was responsible. Clearly, a debate about the role of subsidy in the arts would have been high on their list of conversation topics. "When I took the job, I signed up to Stephen's approach. Like him, I believe passionately that the arts should be part of the fabric of life and not élitist," said Robson. "Some of the best work I've seen would have been impossible without subsidy. But equally, I accept that the greater the degree of self-sufficiency, the stronger The Lowry's position will be. There's already been a large amount of subsidy in the creation of the building. Stephen explained the need to serve the market. If we do that properly, we will be self-sufficient, but there will always be healthy tensions over the relationship between artistic quality and subsidy."

In taking on the broad-ranging theatres remit, Robson was in effect being handed one of the project's stiffest operational challenges because the commercial performance of the theatres will have the greatest financial implications for the running of The Lowry. "A lot of people say we'll never make it add up. It won't be easy but that's the challenge," said Robson. "It will be in our interests to keep the two theatre auditoriums open and running all year round, although there could be a shift of emphasis to more outdoor performance in summer."

The general view was that opera and ballet should be at the heart of The Lowry's performing arts programme. Robson's credo was "residencies, not resident companies", meaning that although The Lowry would have no resident theatre company, it would seek to establish "partner" agreements with major touring companies such as Birmingham Royal Ballet and Opera North to visit The Lowry regularly and be involved in community, education and outreach work.

Preparing the theatres

As Robson set about using his extensive range of contacts with commercial producers, subsidised theatres, local promoters, international agents and arts festivals to start building his programme, so Theatre Projects and acoustic consultants Sandy Brown Associates continued with their work

to make the auditoriums ready for whatever would be booked into The Lowry. To procure and install all the lighting, sound and stage engineering systems required, Theatre Projects prepared all the bid documentation and circulated it to the few specialist companies involved in this type of work. These companies were in great demand because of Lottery money financing so many new arts venues, a position reflected in their prices and lead times.

Working closely with Michael Wilford & Partners, Theatre Projects then checked the production drawings prepared by each contractor, visited their factories to oversee the systems being manufactured, and supervised their installation on site. As the final countdown to the opening of The Lowry began, all of this equipment was commissioned and tested to ensure that it functioned effectively. Theatre Projects also made arrangements to run further technical checks once The Lowry was open. "The theatre industry runs on the grapevine and theatre technicians are hard to please," explained Jeremy Godden. "If the systems don't work all the time, we soon hear about it and so does everyone else."

At Sandy Brown Associates, meanwhile, acoustician Kyri Kyriadikes and his team were wrestling with the various acoustic problems in the building. Having solved the architectural challenge of the low ceiling line in the Lyric Theatre by inserting a perforated metal ceiling through which sound could travel, Kyriadikes installed retractable acoustic drapes above the visual ceiling which would alter the reverberation times and give the main Lowry auditorium the variable acoustics it required. These electrically operated drapes were set on six tracks and acoustic reflectors were also installed above the metal ceiling. The rear "crinkle" wall of the auditorium, designed by Wilford in several sections, was also utilised as a diffusing surface for sound.

Kyriadikes was concerned that even if the Lyric Theatre was half empty, the acoustics should remain the same. Maintaining sound consistency irrespective of occupancy depended on the seating - each seat, properly specified with a soft upholstered fabric, provides the same level of sound absorbency as a person (soft seating is also quieter when people shift in their seats during performances). But as Sandy Brown Associates began to carry out final tests on sound insulation and background noise, Kyriadikes became concerned that the value-engineering exercises being carried out by the building team might result in economies on interior finish with damaging implications for acoustic quality. "If a finish to a staircase outside one of the theatres is compromised, there will be more vibration from people's movements felt inside the auditorium," explained Kyriadikes.

Although some battles were lost amidst a late wave of cost-cutting on the budget for interior finishes, many quality materials were saved. When an expensive building package for stainless steel balustrades landed on David Porter's desk at project management company Gleeds, he was forced to go to The Lowry Centre Trust with Michael Wilford to plead the case for stainless steel in the face of a cheaper option, powder-coated mild steel. Their argument won the day, but it was a near thing. Right up to the wire, the commissioning of the interiors would be a fraught process.

Visual art leader

David Alston's visual art credentials were no less impressive than Robert Robson's track record in the theatre. The new Lowry galleries director, an Oxford-educated art historian, began his career as assistant curator of the Christ Church Picture Gallery in Oxford. In 1982 he moved to Sheffield City Art Galleries to take charge of the rehousing of the Ruskin Collection, first as assistant keeper of art and then as deputy director of arts. After 12 years at Sheffield, Alston moved again to become keeper of art at the National Museums and Galleries of Wales, which has some superb art collections.

Each new post extended Alston's expertise into new areas beyond his original academic specialism in 18th and 19th century French art. Working with the Ruskin Collection in particular was a powerful influence. "Ruskin was my first experience of representing a collection in a new building and seeing how it could all mesh together," explained Alston. "There is also something in Ruskin's messianic mission to salvage something from the industrial revolution which links to The Lowry's art-for-the-people message."

As a visual art curator, Alston says he was always interested in audiences. "There are two types of curator - the academic and the hybrid who wants to do exhibitions. I'm the second type," he explained. "My view is that art is only made when someone looks at it. In the first instance that is the artist. This business of the audience's eye explains my interest in doing exhibitions."

Reassessing Lowry

Alston applied for The Lowry post because of a number of factors. The scale of the project fascinated him; the inclusion of live performance was a draw, given his interest in theatre earlier in his career; he was at a turning point in his work in Wales; and he was attracted by the

Top and centre: Architects from Michael Wilford and Partners present seating options and select colour schemes as part of the interior development of The Lowry.

Above: Galleries director David Alston takes former actress Glenda Jackson MP on a site visit.

Above: The interior of the smaller Quays Theatre is completed and prepared for its first audience.

Opposite: The large Lyric Theatre reflects the intense focus on comfortable seating and good sightlines during design development.

opportunity to think afresh about the work of L S Lowry in the context of the 20th century. "There's an immense interpretative task to look at Lowry again, to get away from the clichéd acceptance of his work," explained Alston, who was himself born in the North-West, in Preston. "The conventional view of Lowry is of busy industrial pictures teeming with people, but I am drawn to the melancholic, ironic side of Lowry, to the very empty seascapes. His work is strong, intriguing, misplaced and doesn't fit in. A lot of art I like doesn't fit in. Lowry is possibly Britain's most popular and most unseen artist. Even those sensitive to his work tend to see him as a provincial. He is misconstrued from all points of view."

Just how badly L S Lowry could be misconstrued as an artist was evidenced by the mixed critical reaction to the news of Salford winning the Lottery award to build The Lowry Centre. Several national art critics sharpened their knives, none more swiftly and pointedly than Richard Dorment in the *Daily Telegraph*, who laid into L S Lowry's reputation the day after the Lottery announcement. But Dorment's attack on the artist's reputation drew a feisty reader response which filled the letters page. "The point about Lowry is that he was not a Titian or a Rembrandt but someone who painted the Lancashire landscape he knew and loved with the single-mindedness of a Cézanne," argued one reader.

According to Mike Leber and Judy Sandling, the Salford Art Gallery curators who between them worked on the L S Lowry collection for 45 years prior to its removal to a new home at The Lowry, "You either love him or loathe him, but he's one of the few 20th-century British artists who people immediately relate to. The artistic establishment have never been able to get to grips with his work, but there really is fantastic interest in it."

Such populism is always destined to have its detractors - and some of the mud being flung was aimed squarely at the newly-erected walls of The Lowry. Brian Sewell, art critic of the London *Evening Standard*, railed against "the utterly risible Lowry Centre, in which the studio sweepings of Britain's worst famous painter are to be venerated in much the same way as our superstitious and ignorant medieval ancestors kowtowed to the thaumaturgical remains of martyrd saints." By the time David Alston joined the team, everyone involved in The Lowry project was looking to him for some form of reassurance on the artist's reputation and a creative approach to how the L S Lowry collection would be represented.

Gail Lord of Lord Cultural Resources, herself a trained art historian, recalled being taken aside by the leader of Salford City Council right at the start of the project and asked: "Tell me, is Lowry really a good artist?" Lord's view was that the Lowry collection of 333 works (55 oils and 278 drawings) could be the jewel in the crown of the new arts centre: "Lowry had a special insight into the identity of the North of England. He had a post-industrial imagination before we ever uttered the word 'post-industrial'." Lord had been party to the Trust's decisions on the visual art side of the project, including the introduction of an L S Lowry study centre alongside the planned sequence of Lowry galleries. Now it was Alston's task to take things on.

Above: Local schoolchildren at Salford Art Gallery learn about L S Lowry by sketching his work.

Opposite: The main structural 'boxes' which form the sequence of visual art galleries under construction.

Access and engagement

When he studied the plans for the building and made his own assumptions about the interior spaces in use, the new Lowry galleries director found himself in a bind. Certain decisions had already been taken which would be hard to undo. But Alston was determined to intervene where he still could. A credible study centre was regarded as essential to attract loans from private

L S Lowry collectors (not all the finest works are in the Salford collection), and to enable researchers to study the artist's work in one place. But Alston nevertheless argued that the study centre in the tower should have some public access and not be reserved exclusively for academics. "I wanted to give the tower more animation," he explained. "I also wanted to orchestrate the circulation route around and above the galleries to avoid museum fatigue where you're shut off from natural light and external views."

Inside the Lowry galleries, as the building team struggled to meet Lord's stringent technical brief for lighting, humidity and temperature controls, Alston began to rethink The Lowry's visual art policy. The Lowry, he declared, should not simply display its own collection and accept touring exhibitions but should actively originate and tour its own shows, in some cases in partnership with other venues. Alston could see the interpretative opportunities - both within the L S Lowry collection, which was due to arrive from Salford Art Gallery, and within the intimate gallery spaces which were taking shape as the building work progressed.

The children's gallery

Although perhaps the scale was new to Alston, the challenge of working with an important art collection in a new building was not. What was uncharted territory, however, was the development of the "children's gallery" which early demographic research had identified as a vital ingredient in the Lowry mix. The project's supporters argued that the "children's gallery" tag was helpful in the campaign to raise money for the total scheme long after the concept evolved into something much more than just for kids. But Alston recognised that tensions might arise in trying to develop an attraction for families with kids that was "midway between an arts-based experience and a leisure experience". Indeed, the early difficulties in planning this gallery reflected his concern.

The starting point for the family gallery, named Artworks, was Lord's discovery that the North-West of England has Europe's highest concentration of children under 15, a fact that is attributed to the region's postwar cultural and religious patterns. In studying the local Lowry catchment area, the Lowry project team linked this statistic to participation rates of families in arts activity in the North-West which were well above the norm. So the idea of a "family gallery" for arts exploration at The Lowry took shape. The problem was what form this should take.

Prior to David Alston's arrival, Stephen Hetherington mapped onto the concept his own views about the role of the arts in unleashing personal creativity within everyone. A leading British exhibition design company, Land Design Studio, was commissioned after a competition to design the children's gallery. But things didn't go according to plan: Hetherington liked Land's spatial concept for the gallery but was unhappy with the lack of definition of content. Land's scheme, in his view, was too architectural and he needed to go elsewhere for content. Bitterly disappointed, Land argued that the concept had never been sufficiently defined. It was a regrettable episode which cost time and left bad blood.

"It was unfortunate, but it was a great learning experience for the Trust," said Gail Lord diplomatically. "When the brief went out to the UK design community, I suppose it was somewhat puzzling. It didn't provide detailed guidance. But really it was a combination of things that sent the project off the rails. The trouble was that although everyone knew what a theatre or a gallery was, nobody knew what a children's gallery should be like." For his part, Hetherington was adamant that giving a tight, prescriptive brief at that point would have been against the spirit of what The Lowry was trying to achieve.

Below: The large structural shell of the Artworks Gallery on the left flank of the building takes shape.

The false start over the Artworks gallery served to highlight different approaches to gallery and exhibition design in the UK. As similar false starts on the zones of the Millennium Dome at Greenwich subsequently revealed, commercial production companies experienced in staging trade shows, pure architectural practices and interpretative design firms with the ability to create narrative experiences within interior space all pitch for exhibition work from very different artistic perspectives, which leads to problems in commissioning and outcomes. Land Design Studio, which worked on the Dome, would consider itself to be in the latter category. But it still fell foul of the tension between spatial form and exhibit content on Artworks. Hetherington would go even further than these distinctions: "We came to realise that exhibition designers couldn't really do it. We needed to find a mechanism to bring artists onto the project."

New designers on board

David Alston was determined not to let things slide. One of the first acts of the new galleries director, even before he joined the project full-time, was to arrange a one-day workshop to pin the project down and name it. By then, however, a new design consultant for the Artworks Gallery was on board - a Canadian firm called Reich + Petch, which was introduced to

the project by Lord Cultural Resources. Based in Toronto, Reich + Petch is a multi-disciplinary design firm specialising in exhibition, interior and graphic design. Its international reputation is based on a number of high-profile projects, including the Canadian pavilion at the 1993 Seville Expo. When The Lowry Centre Trust decided in summer 1998 to address the thorny problem of the children's gallery by reeling in more international expertise, Reich + Petch was on its list.

For partner Anthony Reich, a British architect who had studied at Leicester in the late 1960s and attended lectures given by Jim Stirling, it was a special project which bore the hallmark of a homecoming. "We loved the story and language of the Michael Wilford building, and we met with the architects before our pitch to talk about how we might organise the gallery," said Reich. "When we presented our ideas to The Lowry Centre Trust, we were awarded the project. But it was not as simple as it sounds. After we won the job, we asked Stephen Hetherington what he liked about our proposals and he replied: 'I didn't like any of it.'"

What Hetherington did like was Reich + Petch's desire to act as art directors and creative impresarios in the children's gallery, sourcing ideas and objects from different artists, designers and inventors from round the world, rather than designing everything themselves. Here was the potential solution to the absence of content. It was this flexible, open-minded approach which conceptually unlocked the door to the children's gallery, opening up its potential rather than closing it down in a tight specification. "Reich + Petch's great strength was that their concept was fundamentally different," explained Hetherington. "At this point we needed someone to get it together and make it whole." When this concept was explained to The Lowry Centre Trust in autumn 1998, the gallery planning was given the green light. According to Anthony Reich, "It was a crunch time because there was a credibility issue. The Trust was beginning to wonder whether the goals for the gallery were really achievable."

Artworks takes shape

David Alston's one-day workshop involved all the key players to date in the children's gallery development, including the architects, graphic designers The Chase, Hetherington and Reich. A brainstorming session involved discussion of ideas behind the gallery, the activities that could be envisaged there and which were actively being sourced. This led to a barrage of possible names for the gallery, which needed its own identity within The Lowry and in the outside world. The name Artworks was chosen because of its robustness - "a northern factory feel", according to Alston - and the concept was identified as about breaking down inhibitions and barriers, about a process of a self-awareness through an artistic encounter. In that sense at least, the Artworks gallery was to be a microcosm of the whole building. But Alston recognised the

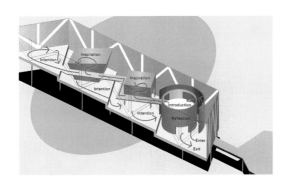

inherent conflict in what was being proposed: "Art does not come about through an easy process, so you can't simplify the questions," he explained. "But, on the other hand, the need to build a robust gallery that will be visited day in and day out drives simple, workable solutions. So there is a tension."

An important constraint on planning Artworks was Hetherington's insistence that there should be no familiar references to art in the facility, no painting or sculpture, image or quotation which might set up a measure by which people could judge themselves as artists. The aim was to create a landscape as free and as abstract as possible to enable visitors to make their own creative connections and contributions, unhindered by precedent. So Reich + Petch proposed an exhibition structure based on four sequential experiences: first, an introductory experience to create self-awareness, set a mood, show that art is a natural and often accidental process, and eliminate the pressure of producing a "perfect" artwork; second, an inspirational experience, to inspire visitors, arouse feelings, enlist participation and enable observation of visiting artists; third, an intentional experience, in which the aim is to interact with a range of exhibits, acquire skills and make art; and fourth, a reflective experience, in which the visitor is allowed moments of introspection to reflect on what they have seen and done, view their own artworks on show and gain confidence about their own creativity.

To achieve this sequence architecturally in the huge gallery space on the left flank of the Lowry building was a difficult task, especially within the £1.2 million budget. "It wasn't just a simple matter of installing exhibitry," said Reich. "We encountered a complex glass-walled shell, three levels high at one end, two levels at the other, that really needed fitting out in terms of all the architectural infrastructure - internal stairs, lighting, landings and so on. But the advantage of Wilford's open approach was that there would be great views of the internal structures from outside."

One of the toughest calls was whether visitors to the Artworks Gallery should go in and immediately up, starting at the top and working their way down, or vice versa. Reich argued that the ascent should be made right at the start of the sequence, with stairs to the upper level supplemented by a lift for disabled access. Working closely with Alston, the designers decided the stairwell should itself preface the introductory experience with light, shadow, clouds and sounds of nature. A Mexican image of creation provided an idea for a spiralling journey through a sound world evoking the experience of nature turning into music and back to the sound of nature.

At the top of the stairs, the visitor encounters an interactive video installation, *Silicon Meets Carbon* by Canadian artist David Rokeby. Sited in the first gallery in the sequence, the piece is intended to intrigue the visitor. It uses the four elements, earth, air, water and fire, each element triggered by a visitor walking around or across a bed of sand. A bridge walkway across the upper level leads

Opposite: The Artworks structure nears completion.

Above: Reich + Petch's exploded diagram shows a sequence of four "experiences" which visitors will encounter along the prescribed architectural route.

to the second room. Alston rejected the idea that this should be a performing space: "We are still at the point with the visitor to Artworks where we are inviting, encouraging participation. We are still on a threshold and need to acknowledge inhibitions." The second room is an immersive environment commissioned from sound artist and composer Volkmar Klien. For the third element along the upper bridge, the Artworks development team decided to organise an international competition among three artist-makers to source a kinetic sculpture - a symbol of the "creative brain". David Kemp emerged from this selection process with his proposal for Creative Brian, a giant walk-through head. You go in one ear and out the other. The brain is worked by visitors below the bridge walkway.

The final room along the top walkway - a room for an "intentional experience" in Reich + Petch's terminology - was designed to engage visitors in making their own art and to take them from the upper level back down to the lower level. A "virtual" colour palette to paint on walls and a system to turn drawings into sound or sound into drawings were described among the attractions. Alston was also keen to "save" the artwork created by families in the gallery by using internet technology to enable young artists to download their creations to their own computer, or print them out to take home, or add them to a "virtual exhibition" on display in The Lowry or on the web at the end of every day. The idea was to build a digital community involved with Artworks but it proved to be a feature which, in the planning stages, remained outside the scope of the available budget.

The final area, the reflective experience, can be found downstairs on the lower level leading back to the entrance, so creating a total circulation flow which owes much to Reich + Petch's experience of building Expo pavilions. "We envisage that the Artworks Gallery will accommodate 80 people very comfortably at any one time," explained Alston. "If there are 150 people in the space, there may be a degree of frustration in waiting too long to try interactive exhibits. There will be a team of enablers on hand to encourage people to use particular exhibits. We anticipate the average family visit will be about one hour and 20 minutes."

With the conceptual and architectural framework finally in place, the final months prior to opening were spent trying to catch up on lost time in the Artworks Gallery, commissioning the exhibitry and building the internal structure. Throughout that time, the debate about what children and their parents would encounter and what they would take away from their artistic "journey" through the gallery never relented. But David Alston relished the intellectual as well as the technical challenge. "The challenge is to get it talked about - without this factor, the visitor projections would be daunting. Artworks is unknown country, which makes it hard, but it is also at the heart of what the whole Lowry experience should be about," he explained. "It is a fundamental ingredient in the democracy of the building."

Development of David Kemp's Creative Brian kinetic sculpture for the Artworks Gallery. Top: The artist presents a maquette of his sculpture to The Lowry team. Centre: An illustration from Kemp's notebook shows how visitors will interact with the giant brain. Right: Installing Creative Brian in the Artworks Gallery.

7 IDENTITY AND AUDIENCE

"Every brand needs to be based on a universal and eternal truth that will stand the test of time without challenge. The Lowry's brand truth is that it opens the door...."

David Bell, Cheetham Bell advertising agency

**The original logo for the project,
featuring L S Lowry's signature
and matchstick men: but was
this the right image to present?**

An outstanding work of architecture, brilliantly engineered and constructed; an exceptional series of interior spaces, skillfully planned and realised; but would the people come? Would The Lowry be able to attract audiences in sufficient numbers to justify its ambitious project? Would the ordinary man or woman in the street, about whom the first Millennium Commission chairman Peter Brooke talked so much, understand its purpose and the mixed nature of its programming?

Questions surrounding The Lowry's identity, branding, marketing and audience profile would assume growing importance the closer the project team came to the grand opening in April 2000. But long before the final countdown was underway, making sure that The Lowry communicated its message effectively was a central concern for chief executive Stephen Hetherington and his team.

The project's origins within Salford City Council had left a visual legacy for The Lowry Centre Trust to ponder. The building was named The Lowry Centre Salford and its visual identity included some famous matchstick men above Lowry's own signature, which was drawn like a meandering band of water. But as Christopher Hulme, company secretary for The Lowry project, observed: "The logo had been successful in raising the project's profile as part of the Lottery bid but did we really want flat-capped, downtrodden, rainswept figures hunched against the biting northern wind to represent a fun day out at a new arts venue?"

Hulme's observation was borne out by a market study presented to the Trust in May 1998 by Arts About Manchester, a local market research agency. Through interviews, surveys and focus groups, this attempted to calculate potential audience numbers for activities at The Lowry and to discover barriers to attendance. While the response to the project was, on the whole, positive - The Lowry was described as having the potential to become the North-West's equivalent to the South Bank or the Millennium Dome or even the Sydney Opera House - Arts About Manchester was also forthright about the barriers. "Lowry", "Centre" and "Salford" were all identified as obstacles to participation. There was a danger that the name might imply that the entire centre was devoted to L S Lowry's work or to interpreting Salford's heritage, rather than offering a much wider scope of arts activity. Salford itself was viewed as working class, dangerous and difficult to penetrate. And the arts centre concept suggested to many that the venue might be élitist or expensive.

A generic quality brand

Arts About Manchester echoed Hetherington's own views by advising that The Lowry should promote itself as a generic quality brand with a wide choice of wares, in much the same way that a department store or major retailer does. It used the example of IKEA to express the mix of quality, affordability and accessibility to which The Lowry should aspire. Just as in buying IKEA furniture or supermarket wine, people needed help and guidance to build confidence and knowledge. Prior knowledge should not be assumed. Market segmentation of potential Lowry visitors ranged right across the board from "innovators" (the most confident group) and "early adopters" (the most image-conscious group) to "laggards" (a group with traditional tastes requiring the reassurance of recognisable names).

The message was clear enough to Robert Robson, as The Lowry's new theatres director devised his programme. "We can't rely on existing arts attenders," explained Robson. "We need to attract and nurture new and irregular arts attenders if we're to make it work." The intelligence gained from the Arts About Manchester market study fed into the final stages of a project to redesign The Lowry's visual identity, which had been initiated back in November 1996 by

Initial ideas from **The Chase** for the visual identity: the problem was finding a single, governing design idea.

Below: Different options for logotypes are developed and assessed at The Chase; finally the three shortlisted designs, right, are chosen for presentation.

Stephen Hetherington. His choice of consultancy was Manchester design firm The Chase, an award-winning practice, the largest in the region, whose client list ranges from the Royal Mail to Preston North End Football Club.

Creating a new identity

The Chase's creative capabilities are exemplified in a book the design firm has published about its own work, in which there is an entire page devoted to a single quotation: "There was once an old Indian craftsman who passed his time carving beautiful elephants. When admirers asked how he created such masterful blocks of timber, he would reply: 'I just cut away the wood that doesn't look like an elephant.'" But if The Chase thought they could simply strip away everything irrelevant to The Lowry to create the new identity, they were to be disappointed. The process of creating the new design would be tortuous and also controversial.

Hetherington, as ever, was clear about the objective: "The whole project is bigger than the memory of Lowry the artist, so we needed an identity that would be more about urban redevelopment and creativity, and would carry the Lowry name less overtly." However, reducing "The Lowry Centre Salford" to "The Lowry" on a new logo was destined to bring Hetherington and his designers into conflict with Salford City Council. The Chase duly found itself right in the line of fire.

According to Lionel Hatch and Peter Richardson, who directed the project at The Chase, the initial omens were good. The timescale allowed to create the new identity was generous, and Hetherington was informal and collaborative as a client, preferring to create a climate for good work to be produced rather than be prescriptive. But the problem was in isolating a single message to provide the visual focus.

The Chase showed the Lowry Centre Trust identities for other arts organisations such as the Crafts Council, with its engraved "C" mark, English National Opera, with its "O" device like peering into an opera singer's mouth, and the Geffrye Museum, with its keyhole symbol denoting entry to its displays of historic interiors. All these identities were not only based on a single idea, they were also well managed in terms of quality and consistency of application. The Lowry, argued Lionel Hatch, would need to do the same. "But we struggled to get one message for The Lowry: it was visual and performing arts, and urban regeneration, and L S Lowry, and a children's gallery. And on it went."

Hatch was also concerned to make the new Lowry identity as modern, accessible and adaptable as possible. "It had to be a living identity. We didn't want to saddle the place with something that couldn't evolve or change." At an initial presentation, The Chase showed several early concept sketches, including, interestingly, a palette or spotlight with geometric shapes which aroused little interest at the time but on which attention would later focus. At a second presentation, three different logotypes for The Lowry were shortlisted for discussion by the Trust. The response was angry and immediate from the Salford City Council representatives. Where were the matchstick men? Where was "Salford" and "Centre"? There were furious demands for their reinstatement, and only Trust chairman Felicity Goodey's cool intervention kept the project on track.

Architect Michael Wilford studied the different options and declared his preference for one which framed the name within an ellipse, a pool-like form which made reference to The Lowry's waterside location. But Wilford also referred back to the earlier elliptical sketch in which geometric shapes - a circle, square and triangle - sat on a palette or spotlight, signifying both the visual and performing arts. Wilford's observation marked a turning point for The Chase, which went back into design development with the ellipse and the geometric shapes. But still it lacked the defining idea to make the identity work. Furthermore, Hetherington pointed out that Korean electronics giant Samsung had just launched its new global identity with the brand name inside a blue ellipse. The Chase needed to come up with something new and special, and the pressure was mounting.

Inspired by the architecture

At last Hatch and Richardson found the visual logic they had been searching for. It was right under their noses - in the clean, geometric forms of Michael Wilford's architectural composition. The pool/spotlight/palette became the site; the triangle became the building. By subdividing the triangle, symbols could be created for different facilities within the building which corresponded exactly to their form and location. These could be colour-coded and be understandable to non-English speaking visitors. As a design idea, this solution had a life of its own. Hetherington and Wilford were both enthusiastic about the potential. As Hatch explained: "It was not overtly about Lowry or about an arts centre. It was adaptable and could respond to whatever The Lowry would do or become over time." The Lowry brand name was placed beneath the ellipse, the logotype

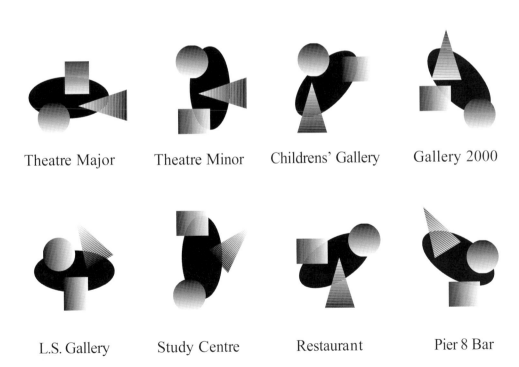

Theatre Major   Theatre Minor   Childrens' Gallery   Gallery 2000

L.S. Gallery   Study Centre   Restaurant   Pier 8 Bar based on an old titling face for inscribed stone called Arrow, but redrawn. The identity was then extended through a range of applications, including signage and sub-branding, to show how it would work. Nearly 20 months after The Chase first started work on the project, the new Lowry visual identity was finally accepted by the Trust. "Sometimes you have to go into enormous complexity just to arrive at a very simple, fundamental solution," said Lionel Hatch philosophically. "It was really there in our first sketch ideas and scribbles."

The identity was unveiled in October 1998, to predictable furore. Local Worsley MP Terry Lewis complained to the *Manchester Evening News:* "Lowry is part of my heritage and it is sad the designer whizz kids have seen fit to drop his signature and trademark matchstick men." Notwithstanding The Chase's impeccable North-West credentials, Lewis remarked: "I smell London influence over this and I don't particularly like it." Councillor Bob Boyd, leader of Salford's Liberal Democrat opposition, saw fit to join the fray: "I can see the argument for not using the word Centre, but the logo as it now stands is characterless."

As ever, media-savvy Felicity Goodey was the rock on which the project could depend. The new logo, she declared, "is modern and classy - the image we want to portray. We want to get away from this 1930s image of Salford - the people of this city deserve better." She was swift to defend The Chase: "It is a brilliant piece of work. It will break down into a whole series of logos - one for each of the theatres and the galleries." And she also made her point about getting away from a parochial image of L S Lowry as a Northern artist: "He is a world-class artist," she told the press.

The brand message

Stephen Hetherington's department store for the arts now had an intelligent and flexible new look which was neither civic nor industrial nor about the downtrodden Northern subjects which populate L S Lowry's art. But, as a brand, would it communicate effectively? Brand strategists would argue that every successful brand has two components: the badge and the message or proposition. For example, BMW has its recognisable marque but it also has a consistent message: "ultimate driving machine". Coca Cola has its signature trademark, but it is also "the real thing". The Chase had created the badge for The Lowry, but what message would be the focus for its marketing?

To discover this, the Lowry Centre Trust drew up a shortlist of three advertising agencies, which pitched for the business in May 1998, at the same time as the Arts About Manchester market report was being published and the visual identity work was reaching its conclusion. The chosen agency was Cheetham Bell, a Manchester "hotshop" with a strong creative reputation which was founded in 1992 by Andy Cheetham and David Bell. Its presentation to the Trust was deliberately

THE LOWRY

conceived to fire the imagination and, importantly, it identified one strong, simple brand message to be communicated.

With the benefit of hindsight, one can argue that things could have been timed differently - that The Lowry's visual badging and brand message should have been worked on simultaneously, that The Chase's struggle would have been easier if they'd be given a brand proposition to work with at the outset. There was a short period of overlap in which The Chase tried briefly to adapt its work to Cheetham Bell's recommendations. But otherwise the two elements of the project remained separate, which was a wasted opportunity.

The design management of the brand identity for The Lowry revealed many things generic to start-up enterprises: the growing need to build brand awareness to attract any kind of audience; the way design can visualise the strategy of an organisation in a form which people can immediately understand and respond to; and the importance of relating the visual image to a core proposition or idea as part of a seamless process of communication. If, during the project, The Lowry didn't always manage to make this process seamless - it designed the flag and defined its message in different corners of the field at different times and required late improvisation to brings things together - then one can say it is not alone in this failing. Many organisations are unable to work the sometimes wayward and unruly inputs of design, advertising, marketing and research into sharp focus; some never even get them facing in the same direction.

The final logotype: a simple solution based on the spatial logic of the building which traditionalists argued was characterless.

Searching for a truth

Cheetham Bell has a proven way of working, according to the agency's co-founder David Bell, a Classical Greek scholar who went into advertising. "Every brand needs to be based on a universal and eternal truth that will stand the test of time without challenge," explained Bell. For its client Pontin's, Cheetham Bell's brand truth was "party, party, party"; for the National Railway Museum, the brand message was "the story of the train"; for Crown Wallcoverings, it was "the home of inspiration". For The Lowry, Cheetham Bell's proposal was "The Lowry opens the door". To support this simple proposition, Cheetham Bell used fast-moving video footage to spell out to the Trust the society in which The Lowry's future customers would be living. "We said that if you want The Lowry to reflect society, then you need to know how the world is changing," said Bell. "It's an 'everything to do, no time to do it' world in which leisure isn't leisurely any more."

The Cheetham Bell presentation painted a picture of the UK with the longest working week in Europe; fewer people doing the same amount of work; lunch as a sandwich at the desk; work running into holidays and weekends and invading the home, blurring the distinction between work and rest; and traditional family days out disappearing. It explored a world in which everything must be done more quickly than before and be immediately accessible - a world of instant loans, one-hour spectacles, disposable cameras, slim-fast, pizza deliveries, drive-through McDonalds, Pot Noodles and rapid-boil kettles; a world in which armchairs aren't for relaxing because there's always a remote control or cordless phone to hand and you can even order an armchair from your armchair via the internet; a world in which there's never "nothing to do" - the leisure choice is overwhelming, from multiplexes, theme parks, paint ball and ice hockey to Mongolian restaurants, vodka bars and cyber cafés.

The Lowry's role in this world, argued Cheetham Bell, was as a counterbalance to long working hours and as a sanctuary from day-to-day pressure. It could put the world in perspective, be a source of mental stimulation and make learning about the arts fun. It was somewhere to escape with a coffee and a book, a creative way to relax. And given what The Lowry had to offer, each person could come to The Lowry for a different reason: for stimulation, enrichment, escape, enjoyment, relaxation, entertainment, discovery and education.

But Cheetham Bell admitted that summing up such a diverse range of experiences wasn't easy. A positioning that tried to encompass everything could end up being too weak; a brand message that said too much could end up saying nothing. A focus on one particular aspect ran the risk of alienating part of The Lowry's target audience, so a solution needed to be found which was relevant to everything on offer at the venue and which allowed each person scope for individual interpretation.

The key to this was to focus on the ability of The Lowry to provide the access to these experiences, rather than concentrating on the experiences themselves. The Lowry was therefore a door to these experiences and out of this thinking emerged the brand message: "The Lowry opens the door". The door, argued David Bell, was a familiar concept to everyone and an evocative one too in terms of arousing curiosity and creating a sense of discovery. Its symbolic overtones were particularly appropriate to the cultural subject matter of The Lowry.

There were other messages within this brand positioning. There was the anti-élitist message: The Lowry opens the door to the arts for everyone, from all walks of society. There was the escapist message: The Lowry is a bolthole from a hectic society. There was the local urban regeneration message: The Lowry opens the door to a new image of Salford. And there was a message that related directly to Michael Wilford's building, which avoids grand porticos

Storyboard from Cheetham Bell's video which communicated the brand proposition, 'The Lowry opens the door', to the Lowry Centre Trust. Like the visual identity, this also took its cue from the building design.

OVERALL BLUE DARK TONES / SOMBER MUSIC TO THIS SECTION.

DARK PASSAGE TO THREATENING DOORWAY

GATES CHAINED UP

VARIOUS SIGNS 'PRIVATE'

CLOSED ETC

PRISON GUARD CLOSING DOOR TO COMPLETE DARKNESS

'It is important to make the buildings open and welcoming... so that people can walk into them'

TITLE SEQUENCE.

MUSIC BRIGHT AND CHEERFUL / COLOURS HAPPY AND VIBRANT.

DOOR BURSTS OPEN BRIGHT COLOURFUL

SIGNS NOW READ OPEN

PEOPLE ENTERING THROUGH AUTOMATIC DOORS

MORE SIGNS.

ANIMATED DOORS FLY OPEN.

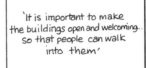

and is itself designed like an open door. Indeed, Cheetham Bell's video used quotations from a Wilford interview on BBC Radio 4 in which the architect observed how so many cultural palaces were intimidating and unwelcoming.

Stephen Hetherington could immediately see the brand potential of "The Lowry opens the door" as a common strapline which could be used on the many different communications tailored to the diverse audience groups for The Lowry. "Our intentions were crystallised in three short words," he remarked. The Lowry now had a brand message or proposition to accompany its brand identity or badge; a rallying cry to go with the flag. Interestingly, both derived at least part of their inspiration from Michael Wilford's open, triangular building by the water. In some ways Wilford was the architect of the entire project, not just the architecture.

Final preparations

To ensure that The Lowry opened the door, on time and on budget, and that people came flooding through it, much still needed to be done. In the final months before opening, the pace quickened even further. A frantic sprint began to complete the building structure, clean up the site, and finish and commission the interior spaces, including the galleries and theatres. The building programme had become squeezed to the extent that the final weeks would turn into a dramatic scramble to the wire. There was some debate over whether the management contract route to building The Lowry was in the final analysis the best way to deliver the building, but post-mortems would be for later. For now, the objective was to hit the deadline.

The artistic programme was finalised and publicised, and the marketing and advertising campaign cranked up. The Lowry's staff shot up rapidly from just 30 people in autumn 1999 to more than 100 people by the time of the opening, many recruited locally. Marketing, box office, gallery, catering, technical and maintenance staff were taken on in a mixture of full-time, part-time and voluntary roles. The Lowry's community and education team, which would be central to the idea of opening the door to new audiences, was established. Named the All Arts Team (because its focus is "Audiences Living and Learning" at The Lowry), this unit was set up to work alongside performing and visual arts staff to break down barriers to access by devising pre-performance talks, master classes, exhibition talks and workshops. The outreach and educational aspects of The Lowry's work was seen as vitally important within Salford City Council right from the first utterances on the project by Bill Hinds and John Willis. Now a key mechanism for delivery on this issue was being eased into place, with a remit to explore arts activities and relationships far beyond the walls and programming of the venue itself.

While Robert Robson worked with his technical manager and team to ensure the proper working order of the stages, David Alston brought in two senior curators to work with him on the visual art side: Lindsay Brooks to manage the L S Lowry collection; Emma Anderson to lead the exhibitions programme. "I must have interviewed everyone in Manchester," declared Alston after a post for a visual arts assistant attracted 172 applicants.

The workload was colossal. "Decisions are coming thick and fast all the time," said Stephen Hetherington. "Everyone is stretched," observed Christopher Hulme. "Trying to live up to all the diverse expectations is incredibly challenging." As if there was not enough to contend with, the final months before opening were further clouded with financial uncertainty. The Lowry project team decided to make a supplementary bid to the main funders in order to deliver the building free of debt. The funders responded positively but went right back to first principles in scrutinising the project. Eventually they were satisfied and granted the top-up funds, but it was an unsettling period for everyone concerned with The Lowry. The Arts Council gave an extra £3.6 million; the National Heritage Memorial Fund added £1 million, and the Millennium Commission diverted £5.3 million from the Digital World Centre project, which was being reworked.

Staff moved over from the small Salford Quays West Pavilion building that was the project team's temporary home for several years, into The Lowry itself. This was a big step. The administration offices were occupied whilst everywhere else was a hard-hat building site. Meanwhile, at Salford Art Gallery, the paintings and drawings of LS Lowry were packed up and prepared for the short journey onto the Quays and into the new building. Works on paper were conserved and remounted. The transfer marked another big step, and a moment Salford Art Gallery curators Mike Leber and Judy Sandling dreaded: "It's like losing a part of the family. To us, Lowry is not just a set of pictures."

THE LOWRY
let the show begin

Events Programme
April – July 2000

The finishing touches were put to the building, just as the finishing touches were put to the artistic programme. The opening festival itself was a year in preparation - each element carefully assembled to make a statement locally, nationally and internationally. As Hetherington explained: "We want the opening to enable the local community to claim the building, to place The Lowry nationally, and to proclaim our international credentials with a major theatrical coup." That coup was the announcement that the Paris Opera Ballet - the oldest and arguably the best ballet company in the world, absent from Britain for 16 years - was coming to Salford during the first week of The Lowry. "I wanted something that was of international significance and that was as prestigious artistically as I could find," said Hetherington. With the British première of *La Bayadère*, Rudolf Nureyev's final production for the company, Paris Opera Ballet was set to catapult Salford Quays to the forefront of European theatre and fulfill Hetherington's ambition to mark the opening with something of international significance and great artistic prestige. Meanwhile a publishing programme initiated by The Lowry Press significantly upped the ante on interpreting and debating Lowry the artist. All eyes focused on Michael Wilford's gleaming structure. But would the building be ready in time? There were anxious moments right up to the end. Then, amid the panic of last-minute adjustments and amendments, The Lowry opened its door.

8 THE BEGINNING

"The grand opening is wonderful but it doesn't mean a thing. It's what The Lowry does for Salford that matters. We're building something more than bricks and mortar; this is really about people and opportunity."

John Willis, Trustee of The Lowry and Chief Executive, Salford City Council

The Lowry opened its door for the first time on the evening of Friday 28 April 2000. Its choice of opening production in the Lyric Theatre was, fittingly, a huge community production, *To You*, directed by Richard Gregory and featuring more than 200 local people working alongside 30 theatre professionals. A challenging and sometimes bleak piece, its crowd scenes were intentionally reminiscent of those in a Lowry painting, albeit in a contemporary Salford setting. *To You* ran for three nights: on Friday, the special guests were the funders; on Saturday, it was the turn of the national arts community; Sunday night was dedicated to local civic leaders. Each night the performance ended outside on the terraces of The Lowry for a spectacular firework display which lit up the Manchester Ship Canal, The Lowry footbridge and the site of the Imperial War Museum - North in dramatic fashion. As the skies rained colour, Felicity Goodey and all around her finally knew the race had been won - but the real work was only just beginning.

Paris Opera Ballet arrived in the main house the following Thursday. Brigitte Lefévrè, who runs the company, told *The Times:* "This season is very important to us. It's been so long and the Paris Opera Ballet needs an international profile - it's never high enough. Plus, you have a new theatre. We have a lot of energy and we hope to bring your new theatre good luck." Opera North and Birmingham Royal Ballet also staged productions within the first couple of months, while Northern Stage Ensemble presented *A Clockwork Orange* by Anthony Burgess. In the Quays Theatre, the first performers on stage were from the Royal National Theatre with *The Oresteia* by Aeschylus. Other companies followed, including dance companies Yolande Snaith Theatredance, Random, Ricochet and Javier de Frutos; drama included the Actors Touring Company with *Macbeth: false memories* by Deborah Levy, and the English Touring Theatre with Chekov's *The Cherry Orchard*.

In the L S Lowry galleries, the opening exhibition based on the collection was entitled *Lowry's People*, which explored the artist's intense emotional portrayal of individuals and crowds. To accompany this, a parallel exhibition entitled *The Double* investigated the idea of identity and self-image behind the portrait through the work of international contemporary artists, Alice Maher, James Rielly, Thomas Ruff and Lindsay Seers. *Urban Panoramas*, a collection of townscapes by Liam Spencer, updated Lowry's interest in documenting the shifting industrial culture of the North-West. There was even a special exhibition explaining the rationale behind the architecture and design of the building. The galleries and promenades were thronged with visitors. In the bars and cafés, people sat and read and talked and admired the views.

Intensity of interest

In the first week of The Lowry, over 70,000 came through the doors to see what was going on,

their interest fuelled by intense national media coverage. Proclaiming a beacon on a bleak landscape, *The Daily Telegraph* declared: "Unlike London's Dome, the piece of architcture already being lauded as 'Salford's Guggenheim', has from its conception been rooted in the fiscal realities of its setting. Other newspapers picked up on the regenerative theme. Paul Barker wrote in *The Independent on Sunday:* "Like Albert Dock in Liverpool, like the Guggenheim in Bilbao, like the Tate Modern which opens on the Bankside shore of Southwark ... The Lowry is a prime example of art being used to pull up an urban landscape, and an urban economy, by its bootstraps." *The Economist*, meanwhile, noted that the project had enabled Salford "to attract the kind of inward investment that the council always hoped for ... the descendants of Lowry's factory hands seem destined to be museum guides".

As critics assessed a landmark new building, only Jonathan Glancey in *The Guardian* struck a discordant note: "What looks like a book of architectural quotations drawn up on a heroic scale by Michael Wilford & Partners is, between its stainless steel covers, an exhausting read." *Harpers & Queen* described it as "without doubt, the sexiest new building in the North." *The Independent* talked of "a shimmering construction that makes structural nods to the vanished historical context."

Making a success

The Lowry began as it intended to go on, full of people, full of things to see and do. But, for the main characters in the story of the making of The Lowry, there was no sense of completion. Instead, the opening of the building was just the beginning. "The grand opening is wonderful but it doesn't mean a thing," said John Willis, Lowry trustee and chief executive of Salford City Council, whose readiness to gamble and determination to win did so much to get the project off the ground. "It's what The Lowry does for Salford that matters. We're building something more than bricks and mortar; this is really about people and opportunity. The Lowry might be a national landmark. The whole world might land on its doorstep - fine. But the real benchmark of success is what the people of Ordsall or Irlam say about this place. It has to be *their* Lowry."

Among the funders of the Lowry project, Millennium Commission director of projects Doug Weston described his own criteria for success: "We hope for good performances in the theatres, lots of people visiting the theatres and galleries, including children in Artworks, and the external spaces used by the public. We also want to see continual regeneration of the area in terms of waterside development." According to Prue Skene, who chaired the Arts Council Lottery Panel, "Of course there have been problems and lessons we have learnt from doing the Lowry project. But I'm glad we did it. It's going to be a fantastic building and a fantastic landmark."

For Lowry chief executive Stephen Hetherington, whose approach did so much to drive up and then meet expectations, the opening left him nurturing a sense of frustration at what had not been achieved. "I never feel the sense of a job well done but that's what I'm like," he said. "But as we finally reach the start line for this extraordinary adventure, the vision for Salford we inherited and then revitalised and strengthened is stronger than it has ever been. This is going to be a lot of fun."

Bill Hinds, leader of Salford City Council, described the realisation of the project as "one of those times in life when everything fits together and you know you're onto a winner. At any other time, it might not have been successful. Take any one of the key people out of the equation and the scheme could have failed...it would have been a hard job without Felicity Goodey and the way she persuaded people; difficult too without Michael Wilford and those who were backing him up." The Lowry's architect in turn paid tribute to his client: "The thing that made us feel confident about this project were the people at Salford City Council. They were determined to make it work come hell or high water."

Overcoming setbacks

The making of The Lowry certainly demanded optimism and fervour in the face of frequent setbacks. The story of its development reveals just what a difficult and complicated project this was to carry through. At the outset, Salford faced the complete closure and dereliction of its docks; scepticism at its vision of urban regeneration; the sudden death of one of its architects, Sir James Stirling, at an early stage of planning; and later, when the Lottery shone a light on the way forward, the mind-numbing complexities of stitching together the funding package.

Above: Local people rehearsing for *To You*, the first stage performance in the Lyric Theatre. Top to bottom: AdHoc dance group; schoolchildren from St Clement's Primary School, Ordsall; choir members in full voice.

In design, engineering and construction, the project overcame a controversially revised masterplan, contaminated ground, an over-budget cost plan, unstable dock walls, complex structural interfaces, awkward sloping walls and exposed steelwork which challenged fire regulations. As the interiors took shape, there were struggles with acoustics in the Lyric Theatre, the concept for Artworks, and the budget for the finishes. Right up to the opening, the branding and marketing of The Lowry was the subject of intense debate and argument. The building completion and handover programme span out of control and fire officers only gave The Lowry a licence at 5pm on the night of the grand opening. Even the funding arrangements were revisited for top-up money to lift the scheme from debt. But then, given the scale of the design and arts management challenges inherent to the project, perhaps one should not be surprised at the catalogue of reversals and the enterprise needed to overcome them.

Herculean managment task

What the story of the making of The Lowry shows any other arts organisation undertaking any scheme with a similar mix of interlocking elements is that coordinating all of these strands represents a Herculean task of design and project management. It is not simply about appointing lots of experts and consultants, lighting the blue touch paper, standing back and letting them get on with it. It is about a continual process of briefing, deliberation, debate and review in which, as Stephen Hetherington described it, "proposals ricochet and rebound back and forth through a forest of ideas and arguments" until the decision is finally made and action taken. Many technical, design and arts consultants on The Lowry project shot ideas into and through this forest, which eventually hit their target. But none could claim sole authorship for different elements of the project. The Lowry Centre Trust, in working through each aspect of the scheme, was the final arbiter in fusing site, locality, community, regenerative purpose, architecture, design, programme, audience and identity into a convincing whole.

Driving it all was Stephen Hetherington's business plan which not only helped to define the functional requirements of The Lowry's many interior spaces but influenced the direction of artistic policy and the focus of marketing. A resident theatre company for the venue was ruled out in the interests of financial self-sufficiency; a large commercial development was ruled in, against the architect's wishes and in contravention of his masterplan, for the same reasons. The self-preservation instinct - the drive to avoid a "lame duck" scenario in which the venue bleeds its local authority and other bodies dry for money to survive - was perhaps stronger than any other on this project. Indeed The Lowry throws new light on the old subject of arts subsidy. At the end of a century in which subsidy became the accepted currency of artistic endeavour, it challenged conventions with a new business model for operation, albeit having based its construction on subsidy from the National Lottery. The Lowry also throws new light on the role of the brand in the arts: once hermetically sealed (largely by virtue of public subsidy) from commercial pressures, arts venues now face the same differentiation and customer loyalty issues as all other businesses. Brand strategy is central to facing these challenges. The Lowry took the necessary steps, sometimes falteringly, down this road.

To You **rehearsals.**
Top: Workmen watch as
choreographer Ruth Jones
works with Axial Dance.
Above: Dance students from
Salford University.

Much has been written about "white elephants" in the arts, created with capital funding generated by the Lottery but unable to sustain their programme due to lack of revenue funding. The Lowry no more wanted to be a white elephant than a lame duck. The business plan was explicit from the start in detailing where the money was going to come from to run the place, and this aspect can

be traced right back up the line to an influence on the primary building design themes of access, openness and engagement. Thus, from the very start, the design of The Lowry was focused on its relationship with the local community and with the North-West catchment area.

Anchor for urban regeneration

Indeed the role of the venue as an anchor for urban regeneration is one of the most compelling aspects of the entire story. In Victorian times, arts and cultural buildings were introduced to urban areas of growing industrial activity and commercial wealth to humanise and complete them, to mitigate the brute forces of business. Today we do the reverse: flagship arts and leisure centres are introduced to urban areas which have lost their industry to reinvent and regenerate them in business terms, to act as a cultural magnet to bring the commercial wealth and investment back.

The catalytic effect of the total Lowry project on a cultural campus which will eventually include Daniel Libeskind's Imperial War Museum - North and the projected Shoah Museum was estimated by 2000 at more than £800 million. It is too early to say if The Lowry will do for Salford what the Staatsgalerie has done for Stuttgart, La Villette has done for Paris, the Port Vell waterfront complex has done for Barcelona, or the Tokyo Edo Museum has done for one large and dowdy district in Japan's largest city. But it is clear that Salford has taken a positive and important step towards a new image for the city which is all-important in a context of growing international competition, culturally and commercially, between cities of a certain rank and status.

One can compare Salford's industrial decline and rebirth with events in Glasgow, a model of regeneration in the 1990s and European Capital of Design and Architecture in 1999, albeit on a smaller scale. In 1993, the year John Willis became Salford's chief executive and really took The Lowry project by the scruff of the neck, Glasgow hosted a world design congress for 1,000 architects and designers, called Design Renaissance. Among its sponsors was the Glasgow Development Agency whose chief executive, Stuart Gulliver, set out his plans for regeneration by the year 2000. "Glasgow is only one of a raft of cities in the industrialised world undergoing radical change - to its economy, to its built form and social patterns," explained Gulliver. "In this transitional period, cities will follow different paths. There will be reactive or 'accidental' cities which take their future for granted and simply react to changing external forces. But other cities will be proactive - 'intentional'. Those cities which are successful will see the city take shape around profound qualitative change rather than quantitative change... successful cities will be good places to live, work and visit. Increasingly, those cities where people of talent and skill choose to live will be those places where businesses will want to be."

Salford City Council has not sat back and simply reacted to external forces. It has been highly proactive - intentional, in the parlance of urban regeneration. The result is The Lowry, set within the quality environment of the redeveloped Salford Quays. The formula is not new - many examples can be cited around the world - but few projects have expressed the idea of an arts flagship pulling up an entire area as vividly and convincingly as The Lowry. Michael Wilford has written: "No architect, however imaginative, can pursue values which are not shared by his client and the community or (are not) within the budget. Significant architecture can only develop from a joint commitment to quality and an understanding of the constraints within which architects have to work."

The Lowry is certainly significant architecture, with a significance which aims to carry far beyond artists and architects to people whose lives are rarely touched by such matters.

A message for the future

The building also marks a rite of passage for Michael Wilford & Partners. "People think that modern architecture doesn't pay enough credence to what has gone before," observed David Alston. "But no matter how radical Wilford's building may appear on the landscape, it has digested history and site. It carries a lot of messages. It is a place where people will want to be." Gail Lord commented that although The Lowry's stainless steel exterior cladding might lead to comparisons with Frank Gehry's Guggenheim Museum in Bilbao, one couldn't compare their functions: "The Bilbao building is wonderful and billowy in design but, as an art gallery, it accommmodates only one function. The Lowry's integration of visual and performing arts makes it a robust and hard-working building, which is very typical of Salford."

Architect Peter Hunter, whose speculative sketch of the Royal Albert Hall on Salford Quays set the ball rolling in the first place, reflected on whether The Lowry could become the Albert Hall of the North-West. "When the Albert Hall opened in 1878, it was considered a monstrous and ludicrous thing to have done. There was a thunderstorm on opening night and people waded across fields on duckboards to get there," said Hunter. "But C B Cochrane, a popular impresario, made it work. Perhaps Stephen Hetherington will be Cochrane's 21st-century equivalent."

The Lowry is a 21st-century building. It is a showcase for creativity at a time when, for the first time, UK earnings from the creative industries of film, design and music now outstrip coal, steel and shipbuilding. But its place on the Manchester Ship Canal is historically significant because it engages with a time when the Canal was a gateway for traditional heavy industries and a "corridor of opportunity". Now it can be again, in a new era of creativity and media. A different age, a different trade, but a new beginning for Salford.

Children from St Clement's Primary School (left) and Salford Youth Orchestra (centre and right) during rehearsals for *To You*.

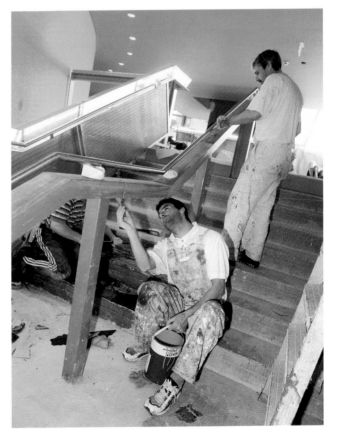

Scenes of frantic work in the final days and hours running up to the deadline to complete and clean up the building before the opening weekend.

The Lowry galleries are
readied for the visitors
under the watchful eye
of Emma Anderson,
curator of the temporary
exhibitions programme
(pictured below).

Above: The right type:
vinyl lettering is installed
in one of the Lowry galleries
as part of the *Lowry's*
***People* exhibition.**

Actors and audience
take their places for the
Salford community
production of *To You*.
This centrepeice of the
opening weekend was
performed in five acts in
and around The Lowry's
main auditorium.

Opposite: Fireworks signal
a spectacular achievement.

Special activities to introduce
children to the building:
reciting poetry (top left);
creating giant heads
(below left);
and painting faces to match
Lowry's portraits (right)

Getting closer to art in
The Lowry galleries.
The installation (bottom right)
is *Candy Cannibal* by
Lindsay Seers.

The building as main attraction. Views along the internal promenade, up the staircase through the sloping wall, and into the cafe near the entrance foyer.

FOR THE LOWRY

Trustees
Felicity Goodey (Chairman)
Bill Hinds
Robert Hough
Joyce Hytner
David Lancaster
John Lawrence, MBE
John Willis

Members
Sebastian de Ferranti
Peter Hunter
Lord Terry Thomas
Michael Unger
David Wilson
Keith Wilson
Chris Yates
Warren Smith

Former Trust Members
Carol Ann Lowry

Founder Patrons
Albert Finney
Ben Kingsley
Sir Peter Maxwell Davies, CBE
Robert Powell
Harold Riley

Capital Funders
The National Lottery through
the Arts Council of England,
the Millennium Commission,
and the Heritage Lottery Fund
European Regional Development Fund
English Partnerships
City of Salford
North West Water
Trafford Park Development
Corporation

Founder Partners
EDS

Architect
Michael Wilford & Partners Limited

Project Managers:
Gleeds Management Services

**Structural, Mechanical
& Electrical Services Engineer**
Buro Happold

Quantity Surveyors
Davis Langdon & Everest

Other Consultants
Theatres
Theatre Project Consultants
Acoustics
Sandy Brown Associates
Galleries
Lord Cultural Resources
Planning Supervisors
Allott & Lomax Consulting Engineers

Site Investigation
Exploration Associates Ltd
Security
Inter Force Assistance
Catering
Tricon
Financial Advisers
Deloitte & Touche
Fundraising
Kalloway Ltd
IT Consultant
Ove Arup
Legal Advisers
Masons Solicitors
Nabarro Nathanson
Cobbetts
Chartered Surveyors
Powis Hughes
Creative Brand Consultants
Cheetham Bell Ltd
Strategic Marketing
Hardsell
Marketing Research
Arts About Manchester
Design Consultancy
The Chase
Design & Advertising
Q2
Public Relations Building Project
Staniforth PR
Kirwin Millard
Public Relations Launch & Opening
Mason Williams
Publishing
Roger Sears

Management Contractor
Bovis Lend Lease

Works Package Contractors
ABB / Haden Joint Venture Limited
Astec Projects Ltd
Best Services Ltd
Broderick Structures Ltd
Cape Industrial Services Ltd
Compass Glass & Glazing Limited
Dane Engineering Ltd
EPH Contracts Ltd
Exterior Profiles Ltd
Heyrod Construction Limited
Irvine Whitlock Ltd
J O Grant & Taylor Ltd
J W Taylor Ltd
Jarvis Newman Ltd
Jim Ennis Construction Ltd
Kvaerner Cementation Foundations
L M Engineering Limited
OTIS PLC
Pennine Telecom
Poltrona Frau SRL
RS Stokvis & Sons Ltd
R Glazzard (Dudley) Ltd
Seceurop UK Ltd
Shawton Engineering Ltd
Survey Operations Ltd
Telestage Associates Ltd

Telling (UK) Ltd
Western Avery Ltd
Widd Signs
William Hare Ltd
Wingate Electrical

Artworks at The Lowry
Architects and Exhibit Design
Reich + Petch Design International
Project & Contract Management
DBA
Lighting Design
Sutton Vane Associates
Visitor Advocacy
Paulette McManus

Digital World Centre
Architects
RTKL
Contractor
Bovis Lend Lease

Lowry Footbridge
Engineer
Parkman
Contractor
Christiani & Neilsen Ltd

Lowry Car Park
Design & Build Contractor
SCC Ltd

Other Services
Banking
Barclays Bank plc
Insurance
Aon Group Ltd

PHOTO CREDITS

Original photography
© Len Grant and The Lowry
Centre Limited except:

p12 (below) courtesy
Edward Gray;
p12 (bottom) and p9
courtesy The Manchester
Ship Canal Company;
p15 (all), p19, p23
(below) and p148
Salford City Council;
p21 Shepheard
Epstein Hunter;
p23 Alistair Hunter;
p25,39,41-45,47-49
Michael Wilford and Partners;
p27 and p37 Hayes Davidson;
p31 Jefferson Air Photography;
p33 Daily Telegraph/Matt;
p45 (bottom)
Roland Halbe/CONTUR;
pp52,53 RTKL;
p55 courtesy of Parkman Ltd;
p63 Buro Happold;
pp66,67 William Cross/Skycam;
p143 Reich + Petch;
p144 (illustration) David Kemp;
pp149-151 The Chase;
p155 Cheetham Bell;
p170 all photographs
Jason Lock.

LEN GRANT would like to dedicate
this work to Daniel, and particularly
to thank the following for their help
during the project: All the construction
workers who have worked on
The Lowry since July 1997 and
especially Peter Roberts and
colleagues at Bovis Lend Lease;
Fairport Engineering Ltd;
Michael Wilford and his colleagues;
Charlotte Cunnah, Tony Struthers and
Jeff Millington at Salford City Council;
Hemisphere Design & Marketing
Consultants; Marshall Walker;
Colourpoint (Manchester) Ltd,
Will Cross of Skycam, Ben Blackall,
Jason Lock, David Wibberley,
Simon Poole at Rochester Kemp Ltd;
Pete Richardson at The Chase, and all
The Lowry consultants and staff.